To

From

Date

My Bible Adventure Through God's Word
52 Bible Stories for Kids
© 2016 by Thomas Nelson

Published in Nashville, Tennessee, by Thomas Nelson. Thomas Nelson is a registered trademark of HarperCollins Christian Publishing, Inc.

Scripture quotations are taken from the International Children's Bible®. © 1986, 1988, 1999 by Thomas Nelson. All rights reserved.

Cover and interior design by Kristy L. Edwards
Illustrations by Doug Jones

ISBN 978-0-7180-9215-3

Library of Congress Control Number: 2016959512

Printed in China

16 17 18 19 20 DSC 5 4 3 2 1

www.thomasnelson.com

My Bible Adventure

THROUGH GOD'S WORD

52 BIBLE STORIES FOR KIDS

Tommy NELSON®

A Division of Thomas Nelson Publishers

Train a child how to live the right way. Then even when he is old, he will still live that way.

—PROVERBS 22:6

Dear Parents,

Life is hectic today, for both children and parents. It is often a challenge to find quiet time each day to spend with God and His Word. This 52-week adventure through the Bible will help you enjoy teaching your child Bible stories about God that will strengthen your child's knowledge and faith in the Lord.

Each week contains a Scripture passage, a devotion, a prayer, and a truth about God for your child to hold on to. Using simple language and beautiful illustrations, this collection offers children timeless truths found in some of the most loved Bible stories in God's Word.

In those quiet moments with your child, share these classic Bible stories, which serve as reminders of God's greatness, love, and care, and will instill His teachings into your child's heart.

Johnny M. Hunt

Dr. Johnny M. Hunt, Senior Pastor
First Baptist Church Woodstock
Woodstock, Georgia

Contents

Week 1   God Made Everything 2
          DR. JOHNNY HUNT
          First Baptist Church Woodstock, Woodstock, GA

Week 2   God Saved the Best for Last 8
          PAM MERCER
          CrossLife Church, Oviedo, FL

Week 3   Pleasing God Is What Matters 14
          DR. MIKE WHITSON
          First Baptist Church Indian Trail, Indian Trail, NC

Week 4   The Flood 20
          DR. BENNY TATE
          Rock Springs Church, Milner, GA

Week 5   Sibling Rivalry 26
          DR. BRAD WHITT
          Abilene Baptist Church, Martinez, GA

Week 6   Stay Close to God 32
          DR. BOB PITMAN
          Bob Pitman Ministries, Muscle Shoals, AL

Week 7   The Boy God Protected 38
               DR. TED TRAYLOR
               Olive Baptist Church, Pensacola, FL

Week 8   God's Good Plan 44
               DR. LARRY THOMPSON
               First Fort Lauderdale, Fort Lauderdale, FL

Week 9   What's in the Basket? 50
               DEBBIE SCHREVE
               First Baptist Church, Texarkana, TX

Week 10   Moses Obeys God 56
               CHRIS BRIDGES
               Calvary Church, Clearwater, FL

Week 11   God Keeps His Promises 62
               KIMBERLY PURVIS
               FBC Temple Terrace, Temple Terrace, FL

Week 12   The Walls Fall Down 68
               DENNIS NUNN
               Every Believer a Witness Ministries, Dallas, GA

Week 13   God's Plan Is Always Best 74
               DR. ROB ZINN
               Immanuel Baptist Church, Highland, CA

Week 14   Samson Prayed to the Lord 80
               PASTOR JEFF CROOK
               Blackshear Place Baptist Church, Flowery Branch, GA

Week 15   God Takes Care of Us 86
               MACEY FOSSETT
               Fossett Ministries, Dalton, GA

Week 16   Did You Hear That? 92
           BEN HUNLEY
           Second Baptist Church, Warner Robins, GA

Week 17   Samuel Anoints Saul King 98
           TIM DETELLIS
           New Missions, Orlando, FL

Week 18   We Need a Hero 104
           DR. ADAM DOOLEY
           Sunnyvale First Baptist Church, Dallas, TX

Week 19   The Wisest Request 110
           AMY DIXON
           Liberty Baptist Church, Dublin, GA

Week 20   God Takes Care of Us 116
           DAVID EDWARDS
           David Edwards Productions, Inc., Oklahoma City, OK

Week 21   A Queen's Brave Decision 122
           DR. GRANT ETHRIDGE
           Liberty Baptist Church, Hampton, VA

Week 22   Job Honors God 128
           DAN AND DEBBIE KUBISH
           NewSpring Church, Wichita, KS

Week 23   The Fiery Furnace 134
           DEANNA HUNT CARSWELL
           First Baptist Church Woodstock, Woodstock, GA

Week 24   Daniel Trusts God 140
           DR. JAMES MERRITT
           Cross Pointe Church, Duluth, GA

Week 25   Jonah Runs Away 146
           PASTOR TIM ANDERSON
           Clements Baptist Church, Athens, AL
Week 26   God Can Do Everything! 152
           REV. AARON M. HOLLOWAY
           Burnt Hickory Baptist Church, Powder Springs, GA
Week 27   A Savior Is Born 158
           STEVE FLOCKHART
           New Season Church, Hiram, GA
Week 28   Growing in Every Way 164
           BRADY AND AMY COOPER
           New Vision Baptist Church, Murfreesboro, TN

Week 29   A Voice in the Desert 170
          DR. MELISSA EWING
          First Baptist Church, McKinney, TX
Week 30   How to Be Happy 176
          JANET HUNT
          First Baptist Church Woodstock, Woodstock, GA
Week 31   Talking to God 182
          DR. DON WILTON
          First Baptist Church, Spartanburg, SC
Week 32   A Lesson in Being Wise 188
          ANN WHITE
          In Grace Ministries, Marietta, GA
Week 33   Lost and Found 194
          ANALISA HOOD AND SUZANNE WALKER
          Mobberly Baptist Church, Longview, TX

Week 34   The Father Who Loves His Children 200
           Dr. J. Kie Bowman
           Hyde Park Baptist Church, Austin, TX
Week 35   Love Your Neighbor 206
           Mary Cox
           North Metro Baptist Church, Lawrenceville, GA
Week 36   Helping Your Friend Have Faith 212
           Dr. Ronnie Floyd
           Cross Church, Northwest Arkansas
Week 37   A Surprising Lunch 218
           Anne Chenault
           First Baptist Church, Chipley, FL
Week 38   Walking on Water with Jesus 224
           Mary Eppl
           First Baptist Orlando, Orlando, FL

Week 39   Who's Afraid of the Big Bad Storm? 230
           DR. D'ANN LAYWELL, *North Richland Hills*
           Baptist Church, North Richland Hills, TX

Week 40   Choose to Enjoy Jesus 236
           HOLLIE HIXSON
           Cross Point Church, Nashville, TN

Week 41   Believing in Jesus 242
           DR. DAVID FLEMING
           Champion Forest Baptist Church, Houston, TX

Week 42   Jesus Changes Everything! 248
           PASTOR KELLY BULLARD
           Temple Baptist Church, Fayetteville, NC

Week 43   Amazing Healing 254
           RYAN HARTZELL
           The Creek Church, London, KY

Week 44   Jesus' Last Meal 260
           DR. PATRICK LATHAM
           First Baptist Church Lawton-Fort Sill, Lawton, OK

Week 45   Who Is Jesus? 266
           NORMA BOWERS
           Flint-Groves Baptist Church, Gastonia, NC

Week 46   The Garden 272
           REV. DAVID RICHARDSON
           First Baptist Church, Creedmoor, NC

Week 47   Jesus Went Through Pain for a Purpose 278
           PASTOR JOHN WELBORN
           Crosslink Community Church, Harrisonburg, VA

Week 48   Jesus Is Missing 284
           Dr. Phil Thomas
           Shiloh Baptist Church, Fort Gaines, GA

Week 49   Phillip Tells the Good News About Jesus 290
           Judy Lee
           There's Hope America Ministries, Cumming, GA

Week 50   Blinded by the Light 296
           Missy Benfield
           Prospect Baptist Church, Albemarle, NC

Week 51   Tell the World About Jesus! 302
           H. Marshall Thompson, Jr.
           Riverstone Community Church, Jacksonville, FL

Week 52   Someone Is Listening 308
           Dr. Michael Cloer
           Englewood Baptist Church, Rocky Mount, NC

Contributors 314
Books of the Bible 318
Selected Verses from the Book of Proverbs 320
The Twelve Disciples 322

Week :: 1 ::

God Made Everything

GENESIS 1:1–15

In the beginning God created the sky and the earth. The earth was empty and had no form. Darkness covered the ocean, and God's Spirit was moving over the water. Then God said, "Let there be light!" And there was light. God saw that the light was good. So he divided the light from the darkness. God named the light "day" and the darkness "night." Evening passed, and morning came. This was the first day. Then God said, "Let there be something to divide the water in two!" So God made the air to divide the water in two. Some of the water was above the air, and some of the water was below it. God named the air "sky." Evening passed, and morning came. This was the second day. Then God said, "Let the water under the sky be gathered together so the dry land will appear." And it happened. God named the dry land "earth." He named the water that was gathered together "seas." God saw that this was good. Then God said, "Let the earth produce plants. Some plants will make grain for seeds. Others will make fruit with seeds in it. Every seed will produce more of its own kind of plant." And it happened. The earth produced plants. Some plants had grain for seeds. The trees made fruit with seeds in it. Each seed grew its own kind of plant. God saw that all this was good. Evening passed, and morning came. This was the third day. Then God said, "Let there be lights in the sky to separate day from night. These lights will be used for signs, seasons, days and years. They will be in the sky to give light to the earth." And it happened.

Our heavenly Father is such a good God. He shows His goodness in so many amazing ways.

In the beginning, God made the universe and the planets, the sun and the moon, the earth and all the plants and animals. God made the whole world, and everything that God made was good. When you look up at the stars at night or watch a hummingbird flap its tiny wings or smell a rose, you can think about God's goodness and how amazing all of creation is.

Just as much as God wants you to know He made the world, He also wants you to know He made you because He loves you. The Bible tells us that He cares about all that He makes, so always remember that He cares for you. The sun that warms the earth, the moon that lights the night, and the food you eat when you are hungry are just a few ways that God reminds you of His goodness and His care for you.

Pray with Me

Dear Lord, thank You that when You created the world it was all good. Thank You for being good and giving me all I need. Amen.

Take It with You . . .

In creation, God gave me all I need.

Dr. Johnny Hunt
First Baptist Church Woodstock, Woodstock, GA

God Saved the Best for Last

GENESIS 1:27–28; 2:7–9, 15–23

So God created human beings in his image. In the image of God he created them. He created them male and female. God blessed them and said, "Have many children and grow in number. Fill the earth and be its master. Rule over the fish in the sea and over the birds in the sky. Rule over every living thing that moves on the earth." . . .

Then the Lord God took dust from the ground and formed man from it. The Lord breathed the breath of life into the man's nose. And the man became a living person.

Then the Lord God planted a garden in the East, in a place called Eden. He put the man he had formed in that garden. The Lord God caused every beautiful tree and every tree that was good for food to grow out of the ground. In the middle of the garden, God put the tree that gives life. And he put there the tree that gives the knowledge of good and evil. . . . The Lord God put the man in the garden of Eden to care for it and

work it. The Lord God commanded him, "You may eat the fruit from any tree in the garden. But you must not eat the fruit from the tree which gives the knowledge of good and evil. If you ever eat fruit from that tree, you will die!" Then the Lord God said, "It is not good for the man to be alone. I will make a helper who is right for him." From the ground God formed every wild animal and every bird in the sky. He brought them to the man so the man could name them. Whatever the man called each living thing, that became its name. The man gave names to all the tame animals, to the birds in the sky and to all the wild animals. But Adam did not find a helper that was right for him. So the Lord God caused the man to sleep very deeply. While the man was asleep, God took one of the ribs from the man's body. Then God closed the man's skin at the place where he took the rib. The Lord God used the rib from the man to make a woman. Then the Lord brought the woman to the man. And the man said,

"Now, this is someone whose bones came
        from my bones.
    Her body came from my body.
I will call her 'woman,'
    because she was taken out of man."

TODAY'S ADVENTURE

After God created the world and everything in it, He made man. People are God's greatest creations because they were made in God's image, which means they were made to be like God. God placed the man in charge of all the things He had made. Just as your mom and dad gave you a name, Adam got to name all the animals. That was a big job!

All the cows and horses and dogs and cats had other cows and horses and dogs and cats to be friends with, but not Adam. He did not have another person to keep him company or to help him. He was alone. So God made Adam a helper, named Eve, so that he would not be alone.

God wanted Adam and Eve to know that, no matter what, there was someone to help them. God has given you someone to always be with you too. It might be your mom or dad or your grandmother or grandfather who takes care of you. God loves us so much that He does not want us to feel alone. And no matter what, just as Adam and Eve could talk to God, we can talk to God and He will listen and take care of us.

Sadly, Adam and Eve did not obey God, and they had to leave the garden. But God was still with them, just as He will always be with you. God loves you! You are never alone!

Pray with Me

Thank You, God, for giving me people who care about me, and thank You for loving me, no matter what. Amen.

Take It with You . . .

God loves me and always wants the best for me. I am never alone!

Pam Mercer
CrossLife Church, Oviedo, FL

Pleasing God Is What Matters

GENESIS 4:2–12

After that, Eve gave birth to Cain's brother Abel. Abel took care of sheep. Cain became a farmer. Later, Cain brought a gift to God. He brought some food from the ground. Abel brought the best parts of his best sheep. The Lord accepted Abel and his gift. But God did not accept Cain and his gift. Cain became very angry and looked unhappy. The Lord asked Cain, "Why are you angry? Why do you look so unhappy? If you do good, I will accept you. But if you do not do good, sin is ready to attack you. Sin wants you. But you must rule over it." Cain said to his brother Abel, "Let's go out into the field." So Cain and Abel went into the field. Then Cain attacked his brother Abel and killed him. Later, the Lord said to Cain, "Where is your brother Abel?" Cain answered, "I don't know. Is it my job to take care of my brother?" Then the Lord said, "What have

you done? Your brother's blood is on the ground. That blood is like a voice that tells me what happened. And now you will be cursed in your work with the ground. It is the same ground where your brother's blood fell. Your hands killed him. You will work the ground. But it will not grow good crops for you anymore. You will wander around on the earth."

Adam and Eve had two sons named Cain and Abel. Cain grew up to be a farmer who grew vegetables. Abel became a shepherd and took care of the family's sheep. The time came for everyone in the family to bring an offering to God. The Bible says that God loves people to give with a smile and be glad that they are giving.

Cain, the farmer, took some of the things he had grown and brought them to God. Abel gave God the best parts of his very best lamb. The Bible says that God was happy with Abel and the gift he brought but not with Cain or his gift. This made Cain very angry. He thought God loved Abel more, but he was wrong. God loved them both the same. Cain was so mad and jealous that he killed his brother.

God knew what Cain had done. He punished Cain because he was not sorry and did not tell Him the truth about what had happened. God told Cain that he would have a difficult time growing vegetables because of his sin. Cain also became a wanderer, never living in one place for very long.

If you have done something wrong, tell God you are sorry and ask Him to forgive you. He always will!

Pray with Me

Father God, please let me always do the things that make You happy. When I make mistakes, let me know that You love and forgive me. Amen.

Take It with You . . .

It is always best to choose to live God's way.

Dr. Mike Whitson
First Baptist Church Indian Trail, Indian Trail, NC

The Flood

GENESIS 6:13, 17–22; 9:8–13

So God said to Noah, "People have made the earth full of violence. So I will destroy all people from the earth. . . . I will bring a flood of water on the earth. I will destroy all living things that live under the sky. This includes everything that has the breath of life. Everything on the earth will die. But I will make an agreement with you. You, your sons, your wife and your sons' wives will all go into the boat. Also, you must bring into the boat two of every living thing, male and female. Keep them alive with you. There will be two of every kind of bird, animal and crawling thing. They will come to you to be kept alive. Also gather some of every kind of food. Store it on the boat as food for you and the animals." Noah did everything that God commanded him. . . .

Then God said to Noah and his sons, "Now I am making my agreement with you and your people who will live after you. And I also make it with every living thing that is with you. It is with the birds, the tame animals and the wild animals. It is with all that came out of the boat with you. I make my agreement with every living thing on earth. I make this agreement with you: I will never again destroy all living things by floodwaters. A flood will never again destroy the earth." And God said, "I am making an agreement between me and you and every living creature that is with you. It will continue from now on. This is the sign: I am putting my rainbow in the clouds. It is the sign of the agreement between me and the earth."

Noah was a very good man, but all the people who lived around him were doing things that did not make God happy. One day God said to Noah, "I am going to send a great flood from heaven to destroy every person and every animal because of the wrong things all the people are doing."

God then told Noah, "I want you to build a big boat. You, your wife, and your three sons and their wives should get in the boat before the rain comes so that you will be safe." God also told Noah to put two of every animal into the boat. Noah put cows, dogs, camels, eagles, elephants, and even skunks in the big boat. He also put food for his family and the animals in the boat.

God then sent a great rain, and it covered the whole world. The water was above the highest mountain. Noah and his family and all of the animals floated around for more than one year in the boat.

When the rain stopped and the ground was dry, Noah, his family, and the animals came out of the boat. God said to them, "I want to show you something." Then God put a rainbow in the sky. It was a sign of God's promise that He will never destroy the world with water again.

You can always trust God's promises!

Pray with Me

Dear God, help me always trust You and believe You always have a plan for me. Amen.

Take It with You . . .

God always keeps His promises, and I can trust Him.

Dr. Benny Tate
Rock Springs Church, Milner, GA

Sibling Rivalry

GENESIS 25:21, 24–25, 27–28;
27:1–4, 15–19

Isaac's wife could not have children. So Isaac prayed to the Lord for her. The Lord heard Isaac's prayer, and Rebekah became pregnant. . . . And when the time came, Rebekah gave birth to twins. The first baby was born red. His skin was like a hairy robe. So he was named Esau. . . . When the boys grew up, Esau became a skilled hunter. He loved to be out in the fields. But Jacob was a quiet man. He stayed among the tents. Isaac loved Esau. Esau hunted the wild animals that Isaac enjoyed eating. But Rebekah loved Jacob.

When Isaac was old, his eyes were not good. He could not see clearly. One day he called his older son Esau to him. Isaac said, "Son." Esau answered, "Here I am." Isaac said, "I am old. I don't know when I might die. So take your bow and arrows, and go hunting in the field. Kill an animal for me to eat. Prepare the tasty food that I love.

Bring it to me, and I will eat. Then I will bless you before I die." . . . [Rebekah] took the best clothes of her older son Esau that were in the house. She put them on the younger son Jacob. She took the skins of the goats. And she put them on Jacob's hands and neck. Then she gave Jacob the tasty food and the bread she had made. Jacob went in to his father and said, "Father." And his father said, "Yes, my son. Who are you?" Jacob said to him, ""I am Esau, your first son. I have done what you told me. Now sit up and eat some meat of the animal I hunted for you. Then bless me."

Have you ever argued with your brothers or sisters? I am sure you don't argue too much! Here is a story of two brothers who were arguing with each other before they were even born.

For many years Isaac's wife, Rebekah, could not have babies. So Isaac prayed to God. God heard Isaac and sent not one baby, but two. Twins! The babies were always kicking and fighting inside of her.

The first son born was all red and fuzzy. Isaac and Rebekah named him Esau, which sounded like their word for "red." The other child had smooth skin, and they named him Jacob, which sounded like their word for "heel." This was because Jacob was holding Esau's heel when he was born.

In those days, when the firstborn son became a man, he received a special blessing from his father. The blessing belonged to Esau, but Jacob wanted it. One day, while Esau was out hunting, Jacob and his mother played a trick on his father, who was old and almost blind. Jacob dressed up like Esau and pretended to be him. His father gave the special blessing to Jacob because he thought Jacob was Esau.

Isaac gave everything he had to Jacob and Esau received nothing. This was not an honest thing for Jacob to do, and his actions caused a lot of trouble. It is always important to do the right thing!

Dear God, help me make choices that are good and honest. Amen.

Take It with You . . .

I will always try to be honest and do the right thing.

Dr. Brad Whitt
Abilene Baptist Church, Martinez, GA

Stay Close to God

GENESIS 32:1–8, 22–28

When Jacob also went his way, the angels of God met him. When Jacob saw them, he said, "This is the camp of God!" So Jacob named that place Mahanaim. Jacob's brother Esau was living in the area called Seir in the country of Edom. Jacob sent messengers to Esau. Jacob told the messengers, "Give this message to my master Esau: 'This is what Jacob, your servant, says: I have lived with Laban and have remained there until now. I have cattle, donkeys, flocks, and male and female servants. I send this message to you and ask you to accept us.'" The messengers returned to Jacob and said, "We went to your brother Esau. He is coming to meet you. And he has 400 men with him." Then Jacob was very afraid and worried. He divided the people who were with him into two camps. He also divided all the flocks, herds and camels into

two camps. Jacob thought, "Esau might come and destroy one camp. But the other camp can run away and be saved." . . . During the night Jacob rose and crossed the Jabbok River at the crossing. He took his 2 wives, his 2 slave girls and his 11 sons with him. He sent his family and everything he had across the river. But Jacob stayed behind alone. And a man came and wrestled with him until the sun came up. The man saw that he could not defeat Jacob. So he struck Jacob's hip and put it out of joint. Then the man said to Jacob, "Let me go. The sun is coming up." But Jacob said, "I will let you go if you will bless me." The man said to him, "What is your name?" And he answered, "Jacob." Then the man said, "Your name will no longer be Jacob. Your name will now be Israel, because you have wrestled with God and with men. And you have won."

Esau was very angry at Jacob for cheating him out of the blessing. He even threatened to hurt Jacob. So Jacob ran away for a very long time. After twenty years, God told Jacob to go back home. Jacob's father, Isaac, was now very old, and Jacob surely wanted to see him again. But he was still afraid of Esau.

Esau had forgiven Jacob many years ago, but Jacob did not know that. He was scared that Esau was going to hurt him. God came to Jacob at night in the form of an angel and began wrestling with him. They wrestled all night long. When the battle was over, Jacob was holding on to God and would not let Him go. That was what God wanted all along. He wanted Jacob to be close to Him and to trust Him. And when Jacob and Esau met, they became friends again!

God loves you, and He will never leave you alone. If you will stay close to Him, He will always lead you in the right direction and help you make the right choices. Be sure to stay close to God.

Pray with Me

Father, help me stay close to You now and as I grow older. I know You will never leave me. Help me never to leave You. Amen.

Take It with You . . .

God loves me, and He wants to be close to me.

Dr. Bob Pitman
Bob Pitman Ministries, Muscle Shoals, AL

The Boy God Protected

GENESIS 37:5–8, 12–13, 18–24, 26–28

One time Joseph had a dream. When he told his brothers about it, they hated him even more. Joseph said, "Listen to the dream I had. We were in the field tying bundles of wheat together. My bundle stood up, and your bundles of wheat gathered around mine. Your bundles bowed down to mine." His brothers said, "Do you really think you will be king over us? Do you truly think you will rule over us?" His brothers hated him even more now. They hated him because of his dreams and what he had said. . . . One day Joseph's brothers went to Shechem to herd their father's sheep. Jacob said to Joseph, "Go to Shechem. Your brothers are there herding the sheep." Joseph answered, "I will go." . . . Joseph's brothers saw him coming from far away. Before he reached them, they made a plan to kill him. They said to each other, "Here comes that dreamer. Let's kill him and throw his body into one of the wells. We can tell our father that a wild animal killed him. Then we will see what will become of his dreams." But Reuben heard their plan

and saved Joseph. He said, "Let's not kill him. Don't spill any blood. Throw him into this well here in the desert. But don't hurt him!" Reuben planned to save Joseph later and send him back to his father. So when Joseph came to his brothers, they pulled off his robe with long sleeves. Then they threw him into the well. It was empty. There was no water in it. . . . Then Judah said to his brothers, "What will we gain if we kill our brother and hide his death? Let's sell him to these Ishmaelites. Then we will not be guilty of killing our own brother. After all, he is our brother, our own flesh and blood." And the other brothers agreed. So when the Midianite traders came by, the brothers took Joseph out of the well. They sold him to the Ishmaelites for eight ounces of silver. And the Ishmaelites took him to Egypt.

Sometimes it's hard to get along with our brothers and sisters. They can hurt our feelings or tease us. This doesn't mean they don't love us. We all say and do things we are sorry about.

But Joseph's brothers were mean. They were also very jealous of him. Joseph had several dreams about how he would one day be more important than his brothers. They did not like hearing that at all. And Joseph was their father's favorite son. They were jealous of the special gifts he received from their dad, like a beautiful cloak made of many different colored cloths. But rather than asking God to help them love Joseph, they wanted him to go away.

First they said, "Let's kill him." But Reuben, the oldest brother, realized that was a bad thing to do. He talked his brothers into putting Joseph into a desert well that had dried up. They agreed, and Reuben planned to come back later to rescue him.

But another brother, Judah, came up with a new plan. Ishmaelite traders were traveling through the desert. What if, rather than killing Joseph or leaving him in the well, they sold him to the traders as a slave? They could make money, and Joseph would be gone for good. So that is just what they did. Joseph's brothers sold him for eight ounces of silver, and the Ishmaelites took him to live in Egypt.

Would Joseph see his brothers again? Yes, but it would be a very long time. God was with Joseph, though, and He always protected him.

Pray with Me

Dear God, help me always be kind to my family. I want to be forgiving and not hurt others. Amen.

Take It with You . . .

God keeps me safe. He loves me and will never leave me.

Dr. Ted Traylor
Olive Baptist Church, Pensacola, FL

God's Good Plan

GENESIS 41:46–47, 49; 42:1–3, 6–8;
45:3–5

Joseph was 30 years old when he began serving the king of Egypt. And he left the king's court and traveled through all the land of Egypt. During the seven good years, the crops in the land grew well. . . . Joseph stored much grain, as much as the sand of the seashore. He stored so much grain that he could not measure it. . . .

Jacob learned that there was grain in Egypt. So he said to his sons, "Why are you just sitting here looking at one another? I have heard that there is grain in Egypt. Go down there and buy

grain for us to eat. Then we will live and not die."
So ten of Joseph's brothers went down to buy
grain from Egypt. . . . Now Joseph was governor
over Egypt. He was the one who sold the grain
to people who came to buy it. So Joseph's
brothers came to him. They bowed facedown on
the ground before him. When Joseph saw his
brothers, he knew who they were. But he acted
as if he didn't

know them. He asked unkindly, "Where do you come from?" They answered, "We have come from the land of Canaan to buy food." Joseph knew they were his brothers. But they did not know who he was. . . .

He said to his brothers, "I am Joseph. Is my father still alive?" But the brothers could not answer him, because they were very afraid of him. So Joseph said to them, "Come close to me." So the brothers came close to him. And he said to them, "I am your brother Joseph. You sold me as a slave to go to Egypt. Now don't be worried. Don't be angry with yourselves because you sold me here. God sent me here ahead of you to save people's lives."

TODAY'S ADVENTURE

Have you ever done something wrong and knew you were going to be in trouble if you got caught? Joseph's brothers had treated him very badly. They knew that if their father found out, they were going to be in big trouble. They were scared, so they lied about what they had done. But the truth always comes out!

The people were very hungry because it had stopped raining and food wasn't growing in the fields. Joseph's brothers traveled to Egypt to find food, and they went to an important man to try to get some grain. But they didn't know that man was their brother! Joseph's brothers didn't recognize him, but Joseph recognized them. He said, "Come close so you can hear me better and see me better. I am your brother!"

Can you imagine how those brothers must have felt when they realized that they were talking to Joseph? Would Joseph be mad? Would he hurt them because they had hurt him? Would he tell their dad?

But Joseph trusted God and knew that He had a plan, even when bad things happened. Joseph told his brothers that he forgave them.

Knowing that God was at work all along saved the day . . . and the brothers.

God, thank You for always taking care of me. Your plan is always good. Amen.

Take It with You . . .

I can trust that God always has a good plan for me.

Dr. Larry Thompson
First Fort Lauderdale, Fort Lauderdale, FL

What's in the basket?

EXODUS 2:1–10

There was a man from the family of Levi. He married a woman who was also from the family of Levi. She became pregnant and gave birth to a son. She saw how wonderful the baby was, and she hid him for three months. But after three months, she was not able to hide the baby any longer. So she got a basket made of reeds and covered it with tar so that it would float. She put the baby in the basket. Then she put the basket among the tall grass at the edge of the Nile River. The baby's sister stood a short distance away. She wanted to see what would happen to him. Then the daughter of the king of Egypt came to the river. She was going to take a bath. Her servant girls were walking beside the river. She saw the basket in the tall grass. So she sent her slave girl to get it. The king's daughter opened the basket and saw the baby boy. He was crying, and she felt sorry for him. She said, "This is one of the Hebrew babies." Then the baby's sister asked the king's daughter, "Would you like me to find a Hebrew woman to nurse the baby for you?" The king's daughter said, "Yes, please." So the girl went and got the baby's own mother. The king's daughter said to the woman, "Take this baby and nurse him for me. I will pay you." So the woman took her baby and nursed him. After the child had grown older, the woman took him to the king's daughter. She adopted the baby as her own son. The king's daughter named him Moses, because she had pulled him out of the water.

Joseph's father and brothers moved to Egypt to escape the famine. Their families grew and grew, and they were known as Hebrews. The Hebrews lived in Egypt for four hundred years. A new king, called the pharaoh, came into power, and he didn't know about Joseph and all he had done for Egypt, so he made all the Hebrews his slaves. To keep the Hebrew families from growing, he ordered that the Hebrews could not keep any baby boys that were born.

One Hebrew couple named Jochebed and Amram had a baby boy. They loved him very much and hid him for three months to protect him from the pharaoh.

When they couldn't hide him any longer, Jochebed made a floating basket, wrapped her baby in a blanket, and put him in the basket. She took the basket down to the Nile River and placed it in the tall grass at the river's edge. Even though she was scared, Jochebed trusted God to take care of her son. His sister, Miriam, stayed by the river to make sure her baby brother was safe.

That day, the daughter of the mean pharaoh went down to the river to take a bath. She heard crying and saw the basket. She was very curious. She sent one of her slaves to get it. The princess opened the basket and was amazed . . . inside was a Hebrew baby!

Miriam then ran to the princess. She asked her if she needed a Hebrew mommy to take care of the baby. When the princess said yes, Miriam got her mommy. Jochebed was able to take care of her own baby!

When the little boy was old enough, Jochebed returned him to the princess. The princess adopted him and named him Moses. She named him Moses because she "lifted him out of the water."

Pray With Me

Dear God, help me be brave. Help me trust You and the plans You have for me. Amen.

Take It with You . . .

I do not have to be scared. God will help me when I am in trouble.

Debbie Schreve
First Baptist Church, Texarkana, TX

Moses Obeys God

EXODUS 3:1–8, 10

One day Moses was taking care of Jethro's sheep. Jethro was the priest of Midian and also Moses' father-in-law. Moses led the sheep to the west side of the desert. He came to Sinai, the mountain of God. There the angel of the Lord appeared to Moses in flames of fire coming out of a bush. Moses saw that the bush was on fire, but it was not burning up. So Moses said, "I will go closer to this strange thing. How can a bush continue burning without burning up?" The

Lord saw Moses was coming to look at the bush. So God called to him from the bush, "Moses, Moses!" And Moses said, "Here I am." Then God said, "Do not come any closer. Take off your sandals. You are standing on holy ground. I am the God of your ancestors. I am the God of Abraham, the God of Isaac and the God of Jacob." Moses covered his face because he was afraid to look at God. The Lord said, "I have seen the troubles my

people have suffered in Egypt. And I have heard their cries when the Egyptian slave masters hurt them. I am concerned about their pain. I have come down to save them from the Egyptians. I will bring them out of that land. I will lead them to a good land with lots of room. This is a land where much food grows. This is the land of these people: the Canaanites, Hittites, Amorites, Perizzites, Hivites and Jebusites. . . . So now I am sending you to the king of Egypt. Go! Bring my people, the Israelites, out of Egypt!"

One day Moses was taking care of his family's sheep near Mount Sinai and saw something strange. He saw a bush that was on fire, but it was not burning up.

God saw Moses coming toward the bush and spoke to him, saying, "Moses, Moses." Moses replied, "Here I am." God told Moses not to come any closer to the bush and to take off his sandals because he was standing on holy ground.

God explained that He was the God of Moses' family from long ago. God said that He had seen the bad things that were happening to the Hebrews, who were also called Israelites, in Egypt. God wanted to help them. God wanted to provide a new and wonderful place for them to live.

God explained to Moses that He wanted him to lead the Israelites out of Egypt. Moses did not think he could do this, but God said to Moses, "I will be with you." Moses asked God, "What if the people say, 'What is this God's name?' What should I tell them?" God said to call Him "I Am."

Moses obeyed God. He went to the Israelite leaders and told them that God was going to rescue them from Egypt and give them a new home.

Dear God, You are powerful. Help me trust and obey You just as Moses did. Amen.

Take It with You . . .

God is powerful. He will give me the strength to trust and obey Him.

Chris Bridges
Calvary Church, Clearwater, FL

God Keeps His Promises

EXODUS 14:8–10, 13–18, 21–22, 26–28

The Lord made the king of Egypt stubborn.
So he chased the Israelites, who were
leaving victoriously. The king of Egypt
came with his horses, chariot drivers and army.
And they chased the Israelites. They caught
up with the Israelites while they were camped
by the Red Sea. This was near Pi Hahiroth and
Baal Zephon. The Israelites saw the king and
his army coming after them. They were very
frightened and cried to the Lord for help. . . . But
Moses answered, "Don't be afraid! Stand still
and see the Lord save you today. You will never

see these Egyptians again after today. You will only need to remain calm. The Lord will fight for you." Then the Lord said to Moses, "Why are you crying out to me? Command the people of Israel to start moving. Raise your walking stick and hold it over the sea. The sea will split. Then the people can cross the sea on dry land. I have made the Egyptians stubborn so they will chase the Israelites.

But I will be honored when

I defeat the king and all of his chariot drivers and chariots. I will defeat the king, his chariot drivers and chariots. Then Egypt will know that I am the Lord." . . . Moses held his hand over the sea. All that night the Lord drove back the sea with a strong east wind. And so he made the sea become dry ground. The water was split. And the Israelites went through the sea on dry land. A wall of water was on both sides. . . . Then the Lord told Moses, "Hold your hand over the sea. Then the water will come back over the Egyptians, their chariots and chariot drivers." So Moses raised his hand over the sea. And at dawn the water became deep again. The Egyptians were trying to run from it. But the Lord swept them away into the sea. The water became deep again. It covered the chariots and chariot drivers. So all the king's army that had followed the Israelites into the sea was covered. Not one of them survived.

Pharaoh, the king of Egypt, was a bad man. The pharaoh was angry with Moses, and he was very mad at God. He wanted to hurt Moses and all of God's people, the Israelites. But God promised Moses that He would protect them from the mean pharaoh and keep them safe.

The people of God began to move far away from Egypt with their families and everything they owned. One day they stopped and camped next to the Red Sea. It was so big that they could not even see the other side.

Then they saw that the mean pharaoh was chasing them. He brought his horses, chariots, and all of his army. The Israelites were very scared. Moses told them not to be afraid. He reminded them that the one true God is a great big God who promised to protect them.

God *always* keeps His promises. Moses told the people that their God would fight the pharaoh and his army for them. God told Moses to raise his walking stick above the Red Sea, and He would part the waters and create a safe path through the sea.

Moses did what God said to do. When he lifted his stick, God kept His promise! Moses led the people of God right through the Red Sea on a dry path. As they were walking, they could see the pharaoh and his army getting closer, but they kept walking until everyone was safe on the other side.

When Moses was sure that everyone was safe, he did as God commanded and raised his stick again. This time God closed the path, and the water came down on the pharaoh's army. Moses and all God's people were safe. God kept His promise!

Pray with Me

Dear God, I love You! Thank You for loving and protecting me. Thank You for always keeping Your promises to me. Amen.

Take It with You . . .

God is a great big God. God promises to help me whenever I need Him.

Kimberly Purvis
FBC Temple Terrace, Temple Terrace, FL

The Walls Fall Down

JOSHUA 6:8–12, 14–16, 20

So Joshua finished speaking to the people. Then the seven priests began marching before the Lord. They carried the seven trumpets and blew them as they marched. The priests carrying the Ark of the Covenant with the Lord followed them. The soldiers with weapons marched in front of the priests. And armed men walked behind the Ark of the Covenant. They were blowing their trumpets. But Joshua had told the people not to give a war cry. He said, "Don't shout. Don't say a word until the day I tell you. Then shout!" So Joshua had the Ark of the Covenant of the Lord carried around the city one time. Then they went back to camp for the night. Early the next morning Joshua got up. And the priests carried the Ark of the Covenant of the Lord again. . . . So on the second day they marched around the city one time. Then they went

back to camp. They did this every day for six days. On the seventh day they got up at dawn. They marched around the city seven times. They marched just as they had on the days before. But on that day they marched around the city seven times. The seventh time around the priests blew their trumpets. Then Joshua gave the command: "Now, shout! The Lord has given you this city!" . . . When the priests blew the trumpets, the people shouted. At the sound of the trumpets and the people's shout, the walls fell. And everyone ran straight into the city. So the Israelites defeated that city.

After Moses died, Joshua was the leader of God's people, who were called Israelites. Joshua was also the leader of the army. God told His people that He had a special place for them to live. But there was a problem. Many bad people lived in the land God wanted to give His people. So God told Joshua to lead His people into the land and make the bad people leave.

The first city God's people came to was Jericho. It was a big city. It had high, thick walls all around it. How could God's people capture Jericho?

God had a special plan. God wanted His people to know that He was strong enough to do anything. So He told Joshua how the army was going to get inside the city. Then Joshua told the people God's plan. The soldiers and priests were to walk around the city once a day for six days. Seven of the priests were to blow trumpets. Other priests were to carry the Ark of the Covenant.

All the people in Jericho probably laughed at and made fun of God's people for six days. But on the seventh day, God's people marched around the city seven times, then they all shouted—and the walls around the city fell down!

Because God gave the people His special plan to capture Jericho and it worked, His people knew that God was with them. God could do anything!

Pray with Me

Dear God, I am glad You are stronger than anything or anyone else. Because You helped the Israelites, I know You can help me do hard things too.

Take It with You . . .

Even if something looks impossible, God can help me.

Dennis Nunn
Every Believer a Witness Ministries, Dallas, GA

God's Plan Is Always Best

JUDGES 6:12–16; 7:1, 19–22

The angel of the Lord appeared to Gideon and said, "The Lord is with you, mighty warrior!" Then Gideon said, "Pardon me, sir. If the Lord is with us, why are we having so many troubles? Our ancestors told us he did miracles. They told us the Lord brought them out of Egypt. But now he has left us. He has allowed the Midianites to defeat us." The Lord turned to Gideon and said, "You have the strength to save the people of Israel. Go and save them from the Midianites.

I am the one who is sending you." But Gideon answered, "Pardon me, Lord. How can I save Israel? My family group is the weakest in Manasseh. And I am the least important member of my family." The Lord answered him, "I will be with you. It will seem as if you are fighting only one man." . . .

Early in the morning Jerub-Baal and all his men set up their camp at the spring of Harod. (Jerub-Baal is also called Gideon.) The Midianites were camped north of them. The Midianites were camped in the valley at the bottom of the hill called Moreh. . . . So Gideon and the 100 men with him came to the edge of the enemy camp. They came just after the enemy had changed guards. It was during the middle watch of the night. Then Gideon and his men blew their trumpets and smashed their jars. All three groups of Gideon's men blew their trumpets and smashed their jars. They held the torches in their left hands and the trumpets in their right hands. Then they shouted, "A sword for the Lord and for Gideon!" Each of Gideon's men stayed in his place around the camp. But inside the camp, the men of Midian began shouting and running away. When Gideon's 300 men blew their trumpets, the Lord caused all the men of Midian to fight each other with their swords! The enemy army ran away to the city of Beth Shittah. It is toward Zererah. They ran as far as the border of the city of Abel Meholah. It is near the city of Tabbath.

TODAY'S ADVENTURE

The Israelites had been ruled by the people of Midian for seven years. The Midianites were mean people, so the Israelites asked the Lord for help. The Lord chose a man to save Israel. His name was Gideon. God visited him in the form of an angel and said, "The Lord is with you, mighty warrior!" Gideon was confused. He asked the Lord, "If the Lord is with us, why are we having all these problems with Midian?"

The Lord said to Gideon, "I will be with you. I have given you strength. Go and save Israel." Gideon said to the Lord, "How can You use me?

My family is the poorest in the tribe, and I am the weakest in my family." The Lord told Gideon, "I will be with you!" So Gideon obeyed the instructions of the Lord and left to free Israel.

While Gideon and his army were camping by the water, the Lord showed Gideon the three hundred men He had chosen to help Gideon fight the Midianites. Gideon divided the men into three groups of one hundred. He gave them clay pots, torches, and trumpets. They surrounded the Midianite camp after the Midianites went to sleep.

Later that night, at Gideon's command, the men blew the trumpets, smashed the pots, and held their torches high. The men of Midian woke up confused and frightened by the torches and loud sounds. They began to fight each other instead of Gideon's army! Israel won the battle because Gideon obeyed God, even when God's plan didn't make sense. The Lord was with Gideon.

Pray with Me

Dear Father, please help me obey Your Word and know that You have a plan and purpose for my life. Amen.

Take It with You . . .

"I can do all things through Christ because he gives me strength" (Philippians 4:13).

Dr. Rob Zinn
Immanuel Baptist Church, Highland, CA

Samson Prayed to the Lord

JUDGES 16:23–25, 28–30

The kings of the Philistines gathered to celebrate. They were going to offer a great sacrifice to their god Dagon. They said, "Our god has given us Samson our enemy." When they saw him, they praised their god. They said,

"This man destroyed our country.
He killed many of us!
But our god helped us
capture our enemy."

The people were having a good time at the celebration. They said, "Bring Samson out to perform for us." So they brought Samson from the prison. He performed for them. They made him stand between the pillars of the temple of Dagon. . . . Then Samson prayed to the Lord. He said, "Lord God, remember me. God, please give me strength one more

time. Let me pay these Philistines back for putting out my two eyes!" Then Samson held the two center pillars of the temple. These two pillars supported the whole temple. He braced himself between the two pillars. His right hand was on one, and his left hand was on the other. Samson said, "Let me die with these Philistines!" Then he pushed as hard as he could. And the temple fell on the kings and all the people in it. So Samson killed more of the Philistines when he died than when he was alive.

When you pray, you are talking to God. And God listens when you talk to Him. What should you talk to God about? Tell God that you love Him. Thank God for your family, friends, food, and your favorite things. You can also ask God to help you. This is what Samson did.

Samson was very strong. He had superhero strength! But even strong people need to pray to God for help. Samson prayed to God not only for help but also for forgiveness. Samson had sinned by disobeying God, and it got him into trouble. He even lost all his strength. No matter what sinful things we do, we can pray to God and ask Him to forgive us and help us just as Samson did.

Samson had been captured by some very bad people called the Philistines. The Philistines did not worship the one true God. They worshipped a false god. They chained Samson to two pillars inside their temple to make fun of him and to make fun of God. But when Samson prayed and asked God to make him strong again, God heard and answered Samson's prayer. Samson pulled the pillars down. All the people who hated God were killed. Samson died, too, but he was a hero for God.

God hears your prayers just as He heard Samson's. What do you need to pray and ask God to help you with? God makes us strong when we pray.

Have you done something wrong and need to ask God to forgive you? God will forgive you because He loves you.

Before you go to bed tonight, talk to God. He is always ready to listen!

Pray with Me

Dear God, thank You for listening when I pray. Forgive me when I sin, and make me strong when I need help. Amen.

Take It with You . . .

God listens when I talk to Him. He hears my prayers. He is always with me.

Pastor Jeff Crook
Blackshear Place Baptist Church, Flowery Branch, GA

God Takes Care of Us

RUTH 2:2–3, 5–11; 4:13

One day Ruth, the woman from Moab, said to Naomi, "Let me go to the fields. Maybe someone will be kind and let me gather the grain he leaves in his field." Naomi said, "Go, my daughter." So Ruth went to the fields. She followed the workers who were cutting the grain. And she gathered the grain that they had left. It just so happened that the field belonged to Boaz. He was a close relative from Elimelech's family. . . . Then Boaz spoke to his servant who was in charge of the workers. He asked, "Whose girl is that?" The servant answered, "She is the Moabite woman who came with Naomi from the country of Moab. She said, 'Please let me follow the workers and gather the grain that they leave on the ground.' She came and has remained here. From morning until just now, she has stopped only a few moments to rest in the shelter." Then Boaz said to Ruth, "Listen, my

daughter. Stay here in my field to gather grain for yourself. Do not go to any other person's field. Continue following behind my women workers. Watch to see which fields they go to and follow them. I have warned the young men not to bother you. When you are thirsty, you may go and drink. Take water from the water jugs that the servants have filled." Then Ruth bowed low with her face to the ground. She said to Boaz, "I am a stranger. Why have you been so kind to notice me?" Boaz answered her, "I know about all the help you have given to Naomi, your mother-in-law. You helped her even after your husband died." . . .

So Boaz took Ruth and married her.

Ruth was a young widow who came to Israel from another land. She came with her mother-in-law, Naomi, so she could take care of her and love her. Ruth showed love and kindness to Naomi.

Ruth went into the fields to gather grain for Naomi and herself. Ruth worked hard, and God helped her.

When a kind man named Boaz noticed Ruth gathering grain, he immediately asked the workers to tell him about her. They told him about the kindness she showed Naomi. This made Boaz happy. He could see that Ruth was a special person.

Soon Boaz began to talk to Ruth himself. He told her that she could gather all the grain she wanted in his field and that he would protect her. Soon, Boaz even made Ruth his wife. God gave

Boaz and Ruth a son, and grandmother Naomi loved the baby very much.

God had an amazing plan for this family. Ruth and Boaz's son became the grandfather of King David, who fought Goliath the giant!

God is always with you, and He wants to take care of you. He wants you to know that He will always give you the things you need.

Pray with Me

Dear God, thank You for taking care of me. Thank You for food to eat and a family who loves me. Most of all, thank You for loving me! Amen.

Take It with You . . .

God had a plan for Ruth's life all along. And God has a plan for me.

Macey Fossett
Fossett Ministries, Dalton, GA

Did You Hear That?

1 SAMUEL 3:1–2, 4–10, 19

The boy Samuel served the Lord under Eli. In those days the Lord did not speak directly to people very often. There were very few visions. Eli's eyes were so weak he was almost blind. One night he was lying in bed. . . . Then the Lord called Samuel. Samuel answered, "I am here!" He ran to Eli and said, "I am here. You called me." But Eli said, "I didn't call you. Go back to bed." So Samuel went back to bed. The Lord called again, "Samuel!" Samuel again went to

Eli and said, "I am here. You called me." Again Eli said, "I didn't call you. Go back to bed." Samuel did not yet know the Lord. The Lord had not spoken directly to him yet. The Lord called Samuel for the third time. Samuel got up and went to Eli. He said, "I am here. You called me." Then Eli realized the Lord was calling the boy. So he told Samuel, "Go to bed.

If he calls you again, say, 'Speak, Lord. I am your servant, and I am listening.'" So Samuel went and lay down in bed. The Lord came and stood there. He called as he had before. He said, "Samuel, Samuel!" Samuel said, "Speak, Lord. I am your servant, and I am listening." . . . The Lord was with Samuel as he grew up. He did not let any of Samuel's messages fail to come true.

God loves when people listen to Him and obey what He says. It makes Him happy because He always knows what is best.

There was a woman named Hannah who wanted to have a baby, but it seemed this would never happen. For a long time she asked God for a son. She promised God that she would teach her son to follow Him. Finally, God gave her a baby boy named Samuel. She kept her promise and sent Samuel to live with a priest named Eli so he could serve God.

One night while Samuel was sleeping, God called his name, but Samuel did not know it was God talking. He thought it was Eli. Three times he heard someone say his name. Each time he went to Eli. Finally, Eli realized that God was talking to Samuel. He told Samuel to listen closely when God talked. Eli wanted Samuel to know how special it was for God to talk to him.

The next time God called Samuel's name, Samuel told God that he was listening. Samuel wanted to obey God, who loved him and told him many things.

Samuel was a young boy who obeyed God. You can listen to God and obey Him too. The Bible is full of God's words, so when we read it, it's like we are hearing Him talk to us.

We can talk to God by praying to Him. God loves it when you talk to Him, and He wants you to obey what He says. You show God you love Him when you listen to Him and do what He asks.

Pray with Me

Dear God, help me listen to You. You know everything, and I know I can trust You. Help me do what You tell me to do. Amen.

Take It with You . . .

God will talk to me if I listen closely. I will obey Him.

Ben Hunley
Second Baptist Church, Warner Robins, GA

Samuel Anoints Saul King

1 SAMUEL 8:7; 9:15–17; 10:1

The Lord told Samuel, "Listen to whatever the people say to you. They have not rejected you. They have rejected me from being their king." . . .

The day before Saul came, the Lord had told Samuel: "About this time tomorrow I will send you a man. He will be from Benjamin. You must appoint him as leader over my people Israel. He will save my people from the Philistines. I have seen the suffering of my people. I have listened to their cry." When Samuel first saw Saul, the Lord spoke to Samuel. He said, "This is the man I told you about. He will rule my people." . . .

Samuel took a jar of olive oil. He poured the oil on Saul's head. He kissed Saul and said, "The Lord has appointed you to be leader of his people Israel. You will rule over the people of the Lord. You will save them from their enemies all around. This will be the sign that the Lord has appointed you as leader of his people."

A long time ago, God helped the Israelites run away from a mean king in Egypt. God wanted His people to live together as one big, happy family without any king to rule over them except Himself. But the Israelites decided they wanted to be like all of the other nations and have a king too.

God talked to the Israelites through a man named Samuel, who was a prophet. When the people told Samuel that they wanted a king, he was sad because he knew God was already their king. God told Samuel that the people did not understand what they wanted, but He would give them a king anyway.

God talked to Samuel about the man He had chosen to be the new king of the Israelites. He told Samuel about the man's family and how he was a powerful warrior who would help the Israelites fight their enemies.

Saul was the man God had chosen to be the king. He was tall and very handsome. Saul came to Samuel because he had lost track of some donkeys and thought Samuel would be able to help find them. But Samuel knew it was time to name Saul as the new king. The custom in those days was to pour olive oil on the new king's head and then say important things to him about the kind of king he should be. This was called *anointing*.

When Samuel anointed Saul, he said, "God has chosen you to be the leader of the Israelites. You will be their king and will rule over them. You will protect them and keep them safe from their enemies." The Israelites were happy because now they had a king of their own.

Pray with Me

Dear God, thank You for listening to me. I know that You care about me and will keep me safe. Amen.

Take It with You . . .

God listens to me and gives me what I need every day.

Tim DeTellis
New Missions, Orlando, FL

We Need a Hero

1 SAMUEL 17:4, 24, 26, 31–32, 48–50

The Philistines had a champion fighter named Goliath. He was from Gath. He was about nine feet four inches tall. He came out of the Philistine camp. . . . When the Israelites saw Goliath, they were very much afraid and ran away. . . . David asked the men who stood near him, "What will be done to reward the man who kills this Philistine? What will be done for whoever takes away the shame from Israel? Goliath is a Philistine. He is not circumcised. Why does he think he can speak against the armies of the living God?" . . . Some men heard what David said and told Saul. Then Saul ordered David to be sent to him. David said to Saul, "Don't let anyone be discouraged. I, your servant, will go and fight this Philistine!" . . . As Goliath came near to attack him, David ran quickly to meet

him. He took a stone from his pouch. He put it into his sling and slung it. The stone hit the Philistine on his forehead and sank into it. Goliath fell facedown on the ground. So David defeated the Philistine with only a sling and a stone! He hit him and killed him. He did not even have a sword in his hand.

TODAY'S ADVENTURE

Have you ever been scared? Have you faced a problem that was so big it felt like there was nothing you could do about it?

As God's special people, the Israelites had several enemies who wanted to hurt them. The Philistines were especially scary because they were good fighters. One soldier, a giant named Goliath, stood facing the army of Israel and demanded that someone come out to fight him. Everyone was afraid, and no one moved. Goliath made fun of God's people, and he also made fun of the true God.

No one would fight Goliath because they were too scared. But then a shepherd boy named David appeared. He was not only brave, but also angry that anyone would laugh at God. When everyone else wanted to run away, David stepped forward to fight Goliath. He was willing to be the hero that Israel needed.

When David ran out to meet Goliath, the giant laughed because David was so small. But David took a stone from his bag, loaded his slingshot, swung it in a circle, and threw the stone toward Goliath's head. The rock hit Goliath in the forehead so hard that he fell face-first to the ground. Israel's enemy was dead, and there was no longer any reason to be afraid.

You will never have to fight a giant like Goliath, but there is a battle you cannot win without a hero like David. Our greatest enemy is sin. There is nothing we can do about it on our own. It hurts us because it separates us from God's plan for our lives. Thankfully, God sent a Hero who was like David, but even better. Jesus defeated sin by dying on the cross for us. If you trust Him and give Him your life, your sins will be forgiven.

Dear God, thank You for sending Jesus to save me from sin. Forgive me when I do bad things. Help me remember how much You love me. Amen.

Take It with You . . .

I can trust that God loves me because Jesus died to save me.

Dr. Adam Dooley
Sunnyvale First Baptist Church, Dallas, TX

The Wisest Request

1 KINGS 3:4–15

King Solomon went to Gibeon to offer a sacrifice. . . . While he was at Gibeon, the Lord came to him in a dream during the night. God said, "Ask for anything you want. I will give it to you." Solomon answered, "You were very kind to your servant, my father David. He obeyed you. He was honest and lived right. And you showed great kindness to him when you allowed his son to be king after him. Lord my God, you have allowed me to be king in my father's place. But I am like a little child.

I do not have the wisdom I need to do what I must do. I, your servant, am here among your chosen people. There are too many of them to count. So I ask that you give me wisdom. Then I can rule the people in the right way. Then I will know the difference between right and wrong. Without wisdom, it is impossible to rule this great people of yours." The Lord was pleased that Solomon had asked him for this. So God said to him, "You

did not ask for a long life. And you did not ask for riches for yourself. You did not ask for the death of your enemies. Since you asked for wisdom to make the right decisions, I will give you what you asked. I will give you wisdom and understanding. Your wisdom will be greater than anyone has had in the past. And there will never be anyone in the future like you. Also, I will give you what you did not ask for. You will have riches and honor. During your life no other king will be as great as you. I ask you to follow me and obey my laws and commands. Do this as your father David did. If you do, I will also give you a long life." Then Solomon woke up. He knew that God had talked to him in the dream. Then he went to Jerusalem and stood before the Box of Agreement with the Lord. There he gave burnt offerings and fellowship offerings to the Lord. After that, he gave a feast for all of his leaders and officers.

One night God appeared to King Solomon in a dream, saying, "Ask for anything you want. I will give it to you." Wow! Anything? He could have asked for power or money. He could have asked to be famous. Instead, he asked for what would help him be the best king for God's people. Solomon asked God for wisdom. He wanted to be a wise king so he could make the right decisions for the people he was ruling, and he knew only God could make him that wise.

God was very pleased with Solomon because he didn't ask for a lot of money, or for a long life, or for his enemies to be destroyed. He asked for something that would help others. God promised Solomon that he would be the wisest king to ever live if he would obey Him and His laws. King

Solomon followed God, and he became known as the wisest of all men!

God wants to give you wisdom just as He gave it to Solomon. You just have to ask Him for it. To ask for wisdom means that you want God to teach you to live a life that pleases Him, to know right from wrong, and to learn how to make good choices. Instead of asking God for things you want like new toys and video games, ask Him for what you need.

If God said the same thing to you that He said to Solomon, what would you ask Him for?

God blessed Solomon because he wanted what God wanted. As you grow up, do all you can to learn what God wants for you. God is waiting to answer your prayers and give you wisdom!

Dear God, give me wisdom as I grow so that I will know how to live a life that is pleasing to You.

Take It with You . . .

God is pleased when I ask Him to teach me how to live.

Amy Dixon
Liberty Baptist Church, Dublin, GA

God Takes Care of Us

1 KINGS 17:10–16

So Elijah went to Zarephath. When he reached the town gate, he saw a widow there. She was gathering wood for a fire. Elijah asked her, "Would you bring me a little water in a cup? I would like to have a drink." As she was going to get his water, Elijah said, "Please bring me a piece of bread, too." The woman answered, "As surely as the Lord your God lives, I tell you the truth. I have no bread. I have only a handful of flour in a jar. And I have only a little olive oil in a jug. I came here to gather some wood. I will take it home and cook our last meal. My son and I will eat it and then die from hunger." Elijah said to her, "Don't worry. Go home and cook your food as you have said. But first make a small loaf of bread from the flour you have. Bring it to me. Then cook something for yourself and your son. The Lord, the God of Israel, says, 'That

jar of flour will never become empty. The jug will always have oil in it. This will continue until the day the Lord sends rain to the land.'" So the woman went home. And she did what Elijah told her to do. So Elijah, the woman and her son had enough food every day. The jar of flour and the jug of oil were never empty. This happened just as the Lord, through Elijah, said it would.

Once there was an evil king named Ahab and an evil queen named Jezebel. They did bad things and did not love God. God wanted them to change, so He sent a prophet named Elijah to talk to them. A prophet is a person who speaks God's words to people and shows them God's plans. God sent Elijah to tell them that because of the evil things they had done, there would be no more rain in Israel for several years.

When the rain stopped, the food could not grow. Because Ahab and Jezebel did not obey God, all the people were hungry. But God took care of Elijah by sending him to a place called Kerith Ravine. Elijah found water there, and God also sent birds to take food to him.

Then God sent Elijah to a town called Zarephath where a woman and her son were very hungry because they were running out of food. The woman and her son thought they were all alone, but God was watching out for them. He made their food last until the rains came again. And the woman and her son shared all they had with Elijah.

God took care of Elijah, the woman, and her son. God also wanted them to have faith in Him, and He wanted them to take care of each other.

God will always take care of you, too, and He wants you to love and take care of your family. Look for ways you can show God's love to your friends and family. That will make God very happy!

Pray with Me

God, thank You for taking care of Elijah and the widow and her son. Thank You for taking care of me and my family. Amen.

Take It with You . . .

God is taking care of me, and He also wants me to take care of others.

David Edwards
David Edwards Productions, Inc., Oklahoma City, OK

A Queen's Brave Decision

ESTHER 5:3–4; 7:1–7, 9–10

Then the king asked, "What is it, Queen Esther? What do you want to ask me? I will give you as much as half of my kingdom." Esther answered, "My king, if it pleases you, come today with Haman to a banquet. I have prepared it for you." . . .

So the king and Haman went in to eat with Queen Esther. They were drinking wine. And the king said to Esther on this second day also, "What are you asking for? I will give it to you. What is it you want? I will give you as much as half of my kingdom." Then Queen Esther answered, "My king, I hope you are pleased with me. If it pleases you, let me live. This is what I ask. And let my people live, too. This is what I want. I ask this because my people and I have been sold to be destroyed. We are to be killed and completely wiped out. If we had been sold as male and female

slaves, I would have kept quiet. That would not be enough of a problem to bother the king." Then King Xerxes asked Queen Esther, "Who is he? Where is he? Who has done such a thing?" Esther said, "A man who is against us! Our enemy is this wicked Haman!" Then Haman was filled with terror before the king and queen. The king was very angry. He got up, left his wine and went out into the palace garden. But Haman stayed inside to beg Queen Esther to save his life. He could see that the king had already decided to kill him. . . . Harbona was one of the eunuchs there serving the king. He said, "Look, a platform for hanging people stands near Haman's house. It is 75 feet high. This is the one Haman had prepared for Mordecai, who gave the warning that saved the king." The king said, "Hang Haman on it!" So they hanged Haman on the platform he had prepared for Mordecai. Then the king was not so angry anymore.

One person who does the right thing can make a big difference!

Esther was a young Jewish girl. She was just like every other young girl her age. Then her life changed when she was chosen to be the queen because she was very beautiful. Can you imagine being chosen to be a king or queen of an entire nation?

Esther's new husband, King Xerxes, was a very rich and powerful king. Anyone who came to him without being asked could be punished—even Esther!

Haman was an evil man who worked for King Xerxes. One day, Esther heard that Haman had a plan to go to war against all the Jews in the land. Since she was a Jew, this meant that she and all of her friends and family would be hurt too. This must have made her very sad and scared.

Even though she was afraid, Esther asked all the Jews nearby to pray for her. She decided she was going to talk to the king, even though it meant she might be punished. Esther had a very nice dinner made for the king, so she could tell him about Haman's plan. Esther was a good queen, and the king was not angry with her. He told her she could have anything she wanted.

Esther bravely told the king about Haman's plan to get rid of the Jews. The king was very angry. He decided to help the Jews and to punish Haman instead.

Only God could place Esther in the right place, at the right time. With God's help, Esther did the right thing and talked to the king, and all the Jewish people were saved!

Pray with Me

Dear God, please help me be brave and do the right thing even when it is not easy. Amen.

Take It with You . . .

God will give me the strength to do the right thing even when I am afraid.

Dr. Grant Ethridge
Liberty Baptist Church, Hampton, VA

Job
Honors God

JOB 1:1; 2:1–4, 6–10; 42:10, 12

A man named Job lived in the land of Uz. He was an honest man and innocent of any wrong. He honored God and stayed away from evil. . . .

On another day the angels came to show themselves before the Lord. And Satan also came with them. The Lord said to Satan, "Where have you come from?" Satan answered the Lord, "I have been wandering around the earth. I have been going back and forth in it." Then the Lord said to Satan, "Have

you noticed my servant Job? No one else
on earth is like him. He is an honest man,
innocent of any wrong. He honors God and
stays away from evil. You caused me to ruin
him for no good reason. But he continues to
be without blame." "One skin for another!"
Satan answered. "A man will give all he has
to save his own life." . . . The Lord said to
Satan, "All right, then. Job is in your power.
But you must let him live."

So Satan left the Lord's presence. And he put painful sores all over Job's body. They went from the top of his head to the soles of his feet. Then Job took a piece of broken pottery. And he used it to scrape himself. He sat in ashes to show how upset he was. Job's wife said to him, "'Are you still trying to stay innocent? You should just curse God and die!" Job answered, "You are talking like a foolish woman. Should we take only good things from God and not trouble?" In all this Job did not sin in what he said. . . .

After Job had prayed for his friends, God gave him success again. God gave Job twice as much as he had owned before. . . . The Lord blessed the last part of Job's life even more than the first part. Job had 14,000 sheep and 6,000 camels. He had 1,000 pairs of oxen and 1,000 female donkeys.

Have you ever been sick on your birthday? Or has it ever rained when you had a picnic planned? Have you ever broken a favorite toy? It's no fun when bad things happen to us. It is hard to understand why they happen.

There was a man in the Bible named Job. He loved God very much, and he obeyed God. One day, God talked to Satan about Job. Then Satan said that Job would hate God if God allowed bad things happen to him. But God knew that Job would love Him no matter what, so He allowed Satan to make sad and difficult things happen to Job. Finally, Job even became sick. He got sores all over his body and they hurt *a lot*.

Job's wife thought he should be angry, but Job was not angry with God. He still loved Him. Job showed everyone that he would honor God even when bad things happened. Job prayed for his friends while he was sick. God made Job better and gave him many good things. Job's life was even better than before. And Job still loved and obeyed God.

God wants us to be like Job. Job honored God even when he was hurting. You can honor God too. You honor God by loving and obeying Him, even when bad things happen. When you honor God, other people can see how great He is.

Pray with Me

Dear God, help me love You and obey You even when I am hurting. Amen.

Take It with You . . .

I can love and obey God even when bad things happen.

Dan and Debbie Kubish
NewSpring Church, Wichita, KS

The Fiery Furnace

DANIEL 3:8–12, 19–22, 26–28

Then some Babylonians came up to the king. They began speaking against the men of Judah. They said to King Nebuchadnezzar, "Our king, live forever! Our king, you gave a command. You said that everyone would hear the horns, lyres, zithers, harps, pipes and all the other musical instruments. Then they would have to bow down and worship the gold statue. Anyone who wouldn't do this was to be thrown into a blazing furnace. Our king, there are some men of Judah who did not pay attention to your order. You

made them important officers in the area of
Babylon. Their names are Shadrach, Meshach
and Abednego. They do not serve your gods.
And they do not worship the gold statue you
have set up." . . . Then Nebuchadnezzar was
furious with Shadrach, Meshach and Abednego.
He ordered the furnace to be heated seven
times hotter than usual. Then he commanded
some of the strongest soldiers in his army

to tie up Shadrach, Meshach and Abednego. The king told the soldiers to throw them into the blazing furnace. So Shadrach, Meshach and Abednego were tied up and thrown into the blazing furnace. . . . The fire was so hot that the flames killed the strong soldiers who took Shadrach, Meshach and Abednego there. . . . Then Nebuchadnezzar went to the opening of the blazing furnace. He shouted, "Shadrach, Meshach and Abednego, come out! Servants of the Most High God, come here!" So Shadrach, Meshach and Abednego came out of the fire. . . . Their hair was not burned. Their robes were not burned. And they didn't even smell like smoke. Then Nebuchadnezzar said, "Praise the God of Shadrach, Meshach and Abednego. Their God has sent his angel and saved his servants from the fire! These three men trusted their God. They refused to obey my command. And they were willing to die rather than serve or worship any god other than their own."

King Nebuchadnezzar was the ruler over Babylon. He had a big, tall, gold statue built. The king commanded that everyone bow and worship this golden statue. Anyone who did not bow and worship the statue would be thrown into the fiery furnace.

There were three men named Shadrach, Meshach, and Abednego who were followers of God. They refused to worship anyone other than God.

People from the village noticed that these three young men would not bow and worship the statue, so they went and told the king. The king became very angry. He told his workers to heat the furnace seven times hotter than usual. He ordered his strongest men to tie up Shadrach, Meshach, and Abednego and throw them into the fire.

The men obeyed and took Shadrach, Meshach, and Abednego to the fiery furnace. The flames were so hot that the strong men throwing them into the fire were killed as Shadrach, Meshach, and Abednego fell into the fiery furnace.

King Nebuchadnezzar went and looked into the fire. He saw *four* men walking around and talking to each other in the fire! They were alive and not harmed. The king shouted for the men to come out of the fire. Shadrach, Meshach, and Abednego were not burned at all and did not even smell like smoke.

The king knew that God had been with them and protected them in the fiery furnace. King Nebuchadnezzar then said, "Praise the God of Shadrach, Meshach, and Abednego."

Do the right thing and follow God, no matter what. He will be with you and protect you because He loves you.

Pray With Me

Dear God, help me keep You first in my life. Give me courage to stand for You. Amen.

Take It with You . . .

Do not be afraid to stand up for what is right. God is always with you.

Deanna Hunt Carswell
First Baptist Church Woodstock, Woodstock, GA

Daniel Trusts God

DANIEL 6:13–23

Then those men spoke to the king. They said, "Daniel is one of the captives from Judah. And he is not paying attention to the law you wrote. Daniel still prays to his God three times every day." The king became very upset when he heard this. He decided he had to save Daniel. He worked until sunset trying to think of a way to save him. Then those men went as a group to the king. They said, "Remember, our king, the law of the Medes and Persians. It says that no law or command given by the king can be changed." So King Darius gave the order. They brought Daniel and threw him into the lions' den. The king said to Daniel, "May the God you serve all the time save you!" A big stone was brought. It was put over the opening of the lions' den. Then the king used his signet ring to put his special seal on the rock. And he used the rings of his royal officers to put their seals on the rock also. This showed that no one could move that rock and bring Daniel out. Then King Darius went back to his palace. He did not eat that night. He did not have any entertainment brought to entertain him. And he could not sleep. The next morning King Darius got up at dawn. He hurried to the lions' den. As he came near the den, he was worried. He called out to Daniel. He said, "Daniel, servant of the living God! Has your God that you always worship been able to save you from the lions?" Daniel answered, "My king, live forever! My God sent his angel to close the lions' mouths. They have not hurt me, because my God knows I am innocent. I never did anything wrong to you, my king." King Darius was very happy. He told his servants to lift Daniel out of the lions' den. So they lifted him out and did not find any injury on him. This was because Daniel had trusted in his God.

God's plan is always better! Sometimes bad things happen, and we have to trust that God will do what is best for us.

Daniel served in King Darius's court, and Daniel loved God. He loved God so much that he prayed to Him three times every day. There were some mean men who did not like Daniel or believe in God. These mean men tricked King Darius into writing a rule that said everyone had to pray only to their king and not to the one true God.

Even with this new rule, Daniel chose to do the right thing. He still prayed to the one true God. The mean men saw that Daniel was not obeying the new rule, and they told King Darius. King Darius was sad when he heard this news because he liked Daniel. But in his land, no rule created by the king could be changed. So he had to throw Daniel into a deep hole filled with lions.

As the king's men were closing the hole with a big stone, King Darius told Daniel that he hoped his God was the one true God and that He would save Daniel. The king was worried that the lions would hurt Daniel, but Daniel trusted that God had a bigger plan for him.

The next morning, King Darius ran to see if Daniel's God had protected him. He called out Daniel's name, and guess what? Daniel answered him! He told the king that God had sent an angel to close the lions' mouths. God did not let the lions hurt Daniel.

God knew that Daniel had made a good choice to pray to Him and trust Him, and He protected Daniel. Pray to God just as Daniel did, and trust Him to take care of you. God always has a plan!

Pray with Me

Dear God, help me trust You even when bad things happen. Amen.

Take It with You . . .

God's plan is always bigger! I need to make good choices and trust Him.

Dr. James Merritt
Cross Pointe Church, Duluth, GA

Jonah Runs Away

JONAH 1:1–7, 10–12, 15–17

The Lord spoke his word to Jonah son of Amittai: ²"Get up, go to the great city of Nineveh and preach against it. I see the evil things they do." But Jonah got up to run away from the Lord. He went to the city of Joppa. There he found a ship that was going to the city of Tarshish. Jonah paid for the trip and went aboard. He wanted to go to Tarshish to run away from the Lord. But the Lord sent a great wind on the sea. This wind made the sea very rough. So the ship was in danger of breaking apart. The sailors were afraid. Each man cried to his own god. The men began throwing the cargo into the sea. This would make the ship lighter so it would not sink. But Jonah had gone down into the ship to lie down. He fell fast asleep. The captain of the ship came and said, "Why are you sleeping? Get up! Pray to your god! Maybe your god will pay attention to us. Maybe he will save us!"

Then the men said

to each other, "Let's throw lots to see who caused these troubles to happen to us." . . . Then the men were very afraid. They asked Jonah, "What terrible thing did you do?" They knew Jonah was running away from the Lord because Jonah had told them. The wind and the waves of the sea were becoming much stronger. So the men said to Jonah, "What should we do to you to make the sea calm down?" Jonah said to them, "Pick me up, and throw me into the sea. Then it will calm down. I know it is my fault that this great storm has come on you." . . . Then the men picked up Jonah and threw him into the sea. So the sea became calm. Then they began to fear the Lord very much. They offered a sacrifice to the Lord. They also made promises to him. And the Lord caused a very big fish to swallow Jonah. Jonah was in the stomach of the fish three days and three nights.

TODAY'S ADVENTURE

Have you ever wanted to run away from home?
Jonah ran away one day because he did not
want to go where God told him to go. Jonah was
supposed to go to the city of Nineveh to preach,
but instead he got on a boat and went to a city
far away. It's never a good idea to try to run from
God.

While Jonah was in the boat, God made the
winds blow, and the water got very rough. The
water was so dangerous that it almost broke the
boat in half. Everybody on the boat was scared.
They even threw cargo into the sea, hoping to
keep the boat from sinking.

Jonah was asleep when the captain of the boat
found him and asked, "Why are you sleeping? Get
up and pray to God and maybe He will save us
from this storm!"

The other men on the boat asked Jonah what he did to cause God to be so mad at him. Jonah told them that the big storm was his fault. He told them to throw him out of the boat so the wind and water would calm down.

The men threw Jonah out of the boat, and at once the storm ended. This caused the sailors to make God a promise that they would do good from then on.

As soon as Jonah was thrown into the water, a big fish swallowed him. Jonah stayed inside the belly of the fish for three days and three nights. God protected Jonah, even when he disobeyed. Jonah told God that he was sorry, and God told the fish to spit out Jonah. Then Jonah obeyed God and went to Ninevah.

Pray with Me

Dear God, please help me to always talk to you and never run away when I am afraid. Amen.

Take It with You . . .

I will always obey God. He loves me even when I am in trouble.

Pastor Tim Anderson
Clements Baptist Church, Athens, AL

God Can Do Everything!

LUKE 1:26–28, 30–45

During Elizabeth's sixth month of pregnancy, God sent the angel Gabriel to a virgin who lived in Nazareth, a town in Galilee. She was engaged to marry a man named Joseph from the family of David. Her name was Mary. The angel came to her and said, "Greetings! The Lord has blessed you and is with you." . . . The angel said to her, "Don't be afraid, Mary, because God is pleased with you. Listen! You will become pregnant. You will give birth to a son, and you will name him Jesus. He will be great, and people will call him the Son of the Most High. The Lord God will give him the throne of King David, his ancestor. He will rule over the people of Jacob forever. His kingdom will never end." Mary said to the angel, "How will this happen? I am a virgin!" The angel said to Mary, "The Holy Spirit will come upon you, and the power of the Most High will cover you. The baby will be holy. He will be called the Son of God. Now listen!

Elizabeth, your

relative, is very old. But she is also pregnant with a son. Everyone thought she could not have a baby, but she has been pregnant for six months. God can do everything!" Mary said, "I am the servant girl of the Lord. Let this happen to me as you say!" Then the angel went away. Mary got up and went quickly to a town in the mountains of Judea. She went to Zechariah's house and greeted Elizabeth. When Elizabeth heard Mary's greeting, the unborn baby inside Elizabeth jumped. Then Elizabeth was filled with the Holy Spirit. She cried out in a loud voice, "God has blessed you more than any other woman. And God has blessed the baby which you will give birth to. You are the mother of my Lord, and you have come to me! Why has something so good happened to me? When I heard your voice, the baby inside me jumped with joy. You are blessed because you believed what the Lord said to you would really happen."

Mary was a young girl who lived in Nazareth. Mary loved God and did her best to obey His Word. She was engaged to marry Joseph, a nice man who also loved God.

Mary had pleased God by having faith and trusting Him. One day an angel visited Mary with an important message from God. The angel told Mary that God was going to give her a baby named Jesus in a very special way. Even though Mary did not understand, she trusted God. She knew God always kept His promises and that He could do anything at all.

The angel also told Mary some news about Elizabeth, one of Mary's relatives. The angel told Mary that Elizabeth was also going to have a baby. Everyone had thought Elizabeth could never have a baby because she was very old. Mary saw this as proof that God could do anything. She was so happy for Elizabeth and wanted to celebrate with her.

Mary went to visit Elizabeth in a nearby town. When Elizabeth saw Mary, Elizabeth could feel her unborn baby jump inside her! Elizabeth called to Mary, "You are the mother of my Lord." Elizabeth shared with Mary what had just happened. Elizabeth's unborn baby jumped because he was near Jesus! Mary was so excited!

Mary and Elizabeth trusted and believed in the Lord. Elizabeth told Mary that she had been blessed by God because she believed in Him and trusted His promises. God will bless you in special ways, too, when you love and trust Him.

Pray with Me

Dear God, I love You! Help me trust and obey Your Word. Please help me remember You are God and You can do everything. Amen.

Take It with You . . .

Because God is God, He can do everything. I will trust Him.

Rev. Aaron M. Holloway
Burnt Hickory Baptist Church, Powder Springs, GA

A Savior Is Born

LUKE 2:1, 4–12, 15

At that time, Augustus Caesar sent an order to all people in the countries that were under Roman rule. The order said that they must list their names in a register. . . . So Joseph left Nazareth, a town in Galilee. He went to the town of Bethlehem in Judea. This town was known as the town of David. Joseph went there because he was from the family of David. Joseph registered with Mary because she was engaged to marry him. (Mary was now pregnant.) While Joseph

and Mary were in Bethlehem, the time came
for her to have the baby. She gave birth to
her first son. There were no rooms left in
the inn. So she wrapped the baby with cloths
and laid him in a box where animals are fed.
That night, some shepherds were in the fields
nearby watching their sheep. An angel of
the Lord stood before them. The glory of the
Lord was shining around them, and suddenly
they became very
frightened.

The angel said to them, "Don't be afraid, because I am bringing you some good news. It will be a joy to all the people. Today your Savior was born in David's town. He is Christ, the Lord. This is how you will know him: You will find a baby wrapped in cloths and lying in a feeding box." . . . Then the angels left the shepherds and went back to heaven. The shepherds said to each other, "Let us go to Bethlehem and see this thing that has happened. We will see this thing the Lord told us about."

Mary and Joseph had to travel very far to a city called Bethlehem. Joseph walked, and Mary may have ridden a donkey because she was going to have a baby. They had to go to Bethlehem to be counted by the government.

When Mary and Joseph got to Bethlehem, it was very crowded. They began to look for a place to stay. Mary was very tired, and she was ready for baby Jesus to be born.

There were no rooms for Mary and Joseph, but they found a place to stay in a building where the animalas were kept. Can you imagine all the animals sharing their home with Mary and Joseph?

Soon Jesus was born. Mary and Joseph were so happy, and they wrapped baby Jesus in cloths to keep Him warm. They did not have a bed, so they laid Him in the manger, which was a box where the animals' food was kept.

In a field nearby, shepherds were taking care of sheep. An angel came to tell them about baby Jesus. God's light was shining on the shepherds so brightly that it scared them. The angel said, "Don't be afraid. I have some really great news." He told them that Jesus had been born and that He was in Bethlehem sleeping in a manger. The shepherds went to find Jesus.

Jesus came to earth as a little baby because God loves you so much, and He wants to be your friend. We can read the Bible and go to church to learn more about Jesus.

Pray with Me

Dear God, thank You for sending Jesus to the earth because You love me and You want to be my friend. Help me learn about You and love You. Amen.

Take It with You . . .

Jesus is God's Son, and He loves me very much.

Steve Flockhart
New Season Church, Hiram, GA

Growing in Every Way

LUKE 2:39–52

Joseph and Mary finished doing everything that the law of the Lord commanded. Then they went home to Nazareth, their own town in Galilee. The little child began to grow up. He became stronger and wiser, and God's blessings were with him. Every year Jesus' parents went to Jerusalem for the Passover Feast. When Jesus was 12 years old, they went to the feast as they always did. When the feast days were over, they went home. The boy Jesus stayed behind

in Jerusalem, but his parents did not know it. Joseph and Mary traveled for a whole day. They thought that Jesus was with them in the group. Then they began to look for him among their family and friends, but they did not find him. So they went back to Jerusalem to look for him there. After three days they found him. Jesus was sitting in the Temple with the religious teachers, listening to them and asking them questions.
All who heard him

were amazed at his understanding and wise answers. When Jesus' parents saw him, they were amazed. His mother said to him, "Son, why did you do this to us? Your father and I were very worried about you. We have been looking for you." Jesus asked, "Why did you have to look for me? You should have known that I must be where my Father's work is!" But they did not understand the meaning of what he said. Jesus went with them to Nazareth and obeyed them. His mother was still thinking about all that had happened. Jesus continued to learn more and more and to grow physically. People liked him, and he pleased God.

Have you ever been separated from your parents? Were you at the grocery store or the park or the mall? Guess where Jesus was when He was separated from His parents? He was at the temple, where people worshipped God.

If you have ever been separated from your parents, think about what happened. Did a toy or candy distract you and cause you to wander away from them? Do you know what distracted Jesus from staying with His parents? God's Word— the Bible! He was listening to the Bible teachers and asking questions. In fact, Jesus amazed His teachers by all that He knew.

When Jesus' parents realized He was not with them, they were very upset and hurried to find Him. They were surprised to see Jesus at the temple talking with and learning from His teachers. Jesus' parents did not understand why He was doing this. Jesus loved His parents so much that He obeyed them and went back home with them, even though He enjoyed being at God's house.

Jesus continued to grow in every way. He grew bigger and stronger. He grew in His friendships with others and with God. One part of loving God is learning about Him at His house—we call it church. And another part of loving God is obeying your parents. Jesus did both!

Jesus came from heaven to show you how much God loves you and to be an example of how to live a life that makes God happy. How can you know what you should do? Read your Bible and obey your parents. You show God how much you love Him when you do what He has asked you to do and when you want to learn more about Him.

Pray with Me

Dear God, thank You for sending Your Son, Jesus, to show me how much You love me and to teach me how to love You back. Amen.

Take It with You . . .

I can ask my parents, my teachers, and my pastor questions I have about God.

Brady and Amy Cooper
New Vision Baptist Church, Murfreesboro, TN

A Voice in the Desert

MATTHEW 3:1–6, 11–17

About that time John the Baptist came and began preaching in the desert area of Judea. John said, "Change your hearts and lives because the kingdom of heaven is coming soon." John the Baptist is the one Isaiah the prophet was talking about. Isaiah said:

"This is a voice of a man
    who calls out in the desert:
'Prepare the way for the Lord.
    Make the road straight for him.'"

John's clothes were made from camel's hair. He wore a leather belt around his waist. For food, he ate locusts and wild honey. Many people went to hear John preach. They came from Jerusalem and all Judea and all the area around the Jordan River. They told of the sins they had done, and John baptized them in the Jordan River. . . . "I baptize you with water to show that your hearts and lives have changed. But there is one

coming later who is greater than I am. I am not good enough to carry his sandals. He will baptize you with the Holy Spirit and with fire. He will come ready to clean the grain. He will separate the good grain from the chaff. He will put the good part of the grain into his barn. And he will burn the chaff with a fire that cannot be put out." At that time Jesus came from Galilee to the Jordan River. He came to John and wanted John to baptize him. But John tried to stop him. John said, "Why do you come to me to be baptized? I should be baptized by you!" Jesus answered, "Let it be this way for now. We should do all things that are right." So John agreed to baptize Jesus. Jesus was baptized and came up out of the water. Heaven opened, and he saw God's Spirit coming down on him like a dove. And a voice spoke from heaven. The voice said, "This is my Son and I love him. I am very pleased with him."

God has a plan for your life just as He had a plan for John the Baptist. John the Baptist had an important message from God to share with the people. The Bible says John lived in the desert. He wore unusual clothing and ate strange food. In fact, people probably thought John was a little odd.

John did not care what people thought because he knew God had a plan for his life. From the time John was born, he knew that God wanted him to do something very special.

John was a messenger for God. He told the people that God was sending a special Savior to the world. John shouted in the desert and told the people to get ready for the Savior to come. When people believed John's message and were sorry for their sins, he baptized them in the river.

One day Jesus came to see John when he was baptizing people at the Jordan River. John was happy to see Jesus, but he was really surprised when Jesus asked him to baptize Him. At first, John did not want to do it, but Jesus told him that this was God's plan. Just as he had been doing his whole life, John obeyed and he baptized Jesus. God's Spirit came down like a dove, and God said that He was pleased with His Son. Jesus the Savior had finally arrived.

God must have been happy with John too. John obeyed God his whole life. He followed God and was so happy to prepare the way for Jesus. He was glad to be God's messenger in the desert.

You can also be God's messenger. Tell your friends about Jesus and how much He loves them!

Pray with Me

Dear God, help me remember to obey You. Show me Your plan for my life and help me follow You. Amen.

Take It with You . . .

God has a plan for me and wants me to obey and follow Him every day.

Dr. Melissa Ewing
First Baptist Church, McKinney, TX

How to Be Happy

MATTHEW 5:3–12

Those people who know they have great spiritual needs are happy. The kingdom of heaven belongs to them. Those who are sad now are happy. God will comfort them. Those who are humble are happy. The earth will belong to them. Those who want to do right more than anything else are happy. God will fully satisfy them. Those who give mercy to others are happy. Mercy will be given to them. Those who

are pure in their thinking are happy. They
will be with God. Those who work to bring
peace are happy. God will call them his sons.
Those who are treated badly for doing good
are happy. The kingdom of heaven belongs to
them. "People will say bad things about you

and hurt you. They will lie and say all kinds of evil things about you because you follow me. But when they do these things to you, you are happy. Rejoice and be glad. You have a great reward waiting for you in heaven. People did the same evil things to the prophets who lived before you."

One day Jesus was walking along with His friends and came to a large hill where many people were gathered. They all wanted to hear Jesus teach. Jesus knew that many people were not happy. He taught them some very important lessons about how to live and love other people. Here are some things He taught that you can do that will help you follow Jesus:

- Always put God first and remember how much you need His love and forgiveness.
- If someone you know gets hurt or is sick, pray for that person and ask God to comfort him or her.
- Be kind to everyone, and do nice things for people.

- When you are playing games with your friends, you should always play fair.
- If someone hurts you, forgive that person.
- Listen to music, read books, and watch movies about Jesus, and you will have a happy heart.
- Help your friends get along with each other and love one another. This shows that you love Jesus.
- If friends try to get you to do something that you know you shouldn't do, you should still obey God. When you say no, they might make fun of you. But Jesus will give you a happy heart for doing what pleases Him and not what pleases others.

Jesus wants you to live a happy life. Serving and loving Jesus will help you be happy because He always knows what is good for you.

Pray with Me

Dear God, thank You for giving us the Bible so we can learn how to be happy. Please help me be more like You today and every day. Amen.

Take It with You . . .

Be thankful. Be kind. Be loving. Be happy.

Janet Hunt
First Baptist Church Woodstock, Woodstock, GA

Talking to God

MATTHEW 6:5–18

When you pray, don't be like the hypocrites. They love to stand in the synagogues and on the street corners and pray loudly. They want people to see them pray. I tell you the truth. They already have their full reward. When you pray, you should go into your room and close the door. Then pray to your Father who cannot be seen. Your Father can see what is done in secret, and he will reward you. And when you pray, don't be like those people who don't know God. They continue saying things that mean nothing. They think that God will hear them because of the many things they say. Don't be like them. Your Father knows the things you need before you ask him. So when you pray, you should pray like this:

'Our Father in heaven,
   we pray that your name will always be
   kept holy.

We pray that your kingdom will come.
We pray that what you want will be done,
here on earth as it is in heaven.
Give us the food we need for each day.
Forgive the sins we have done,
just as we have forgiven those who did
    wrong to us.
And do not cause us to be tested;
but save us from the Evil One.'
[The kingdom, the power, and the glory
    are yours forever. Amen.]

Yes, if you forgive others for the things they
do wrong, then your Father in heaven will
also forgive you for the things you do wrong.
But if you don't forgive the wrongs of others,
then your Father in heaven will not forgive the
wrong things you do. When you give up eating,
don't put on a sad face like the hypocrites.
They make their faces look strange to show
people that they are giving up eating. I tell you

the truth, those hypocrites already have their full reward. So when you give up eating, comb your hair and wash your face. Then people will not know that you are giving up eating. But your Father, whom you cannot see, will see you. Your Father sees what is done in secret, and he will reward you."

TODAY'S ADVENTURE

Little boys and girls are very precious to the Lord Jesus. He loves you very much, and He loves for you to talk with Him.

There were a lot of people who followed Jesus everywhere He went. They watched Him all the time and saw the wonderful things He was doing. They wanted to be near Him all the time. They wanted to know how to talk to Him so He would listen and help them.

So Jesus told them how to pray. When we pray, Jesus said we should always say thank You to God for all He has done for us. We should tell Him that we are sorry for the wrong things we have done. Jesus also wants us to forgive anyone who has hurt us. You can ask Him about anything, and you can tell Him about everything in your heart.

There are no special words you have to say or a special place you have to go to talk to Jesus. He is with you all the time, and you can always talk with Him!

Jesus wants you to know that God is listening to you. He loves you and will help you whenever you ask Him to.

Dear God, help me remember to always talk to You. Thank You for always hearing me. Amen.

Take It with You . . .

I can pray to God about anything. He will always listen and answer.

Dr. Don Wilton
First Baptist Church, Spartanburg, SC

A Lesson in Being Wise

MATTHEW 7:24–29

Everyone who hears these things I say and obeys them is like a wise man. The wise man built his house on rock. It rained hard and the water rose. The winds blew and hit that house. But the house did not fall, because the house was built on rock. But the person who hears the things I teach and does not obey them is like a foolish man. The foolish man built his house on sand. It rained hard, the water rose, and the winds blew and hit that house. And the house fell with a big crash." When Jesus finished saying these things, the people were amazed at his teaching. Jesus did not teach like their teachers of the law. He taught like a person who had authority.

One day Jesus was walking along the Sea of Galilee. He looked around and saw lots of people following Him. So He sat down on the side of a hill and began to teach the people.

Jesus taught many lessons on being loving, kind, honest, and forgiving. He told His followers a story about a wise builder. He wanted everyone to understand that—if they listened carefully and obeyed His teaching—they would be wise, just like the wise builder.

There once were two builders who built their houses in different places. Both builders were

probably
taught
that they
must
build
their
houses
on hard
ground, but
only one of
them did so.
He was known as the wise builder because he took
his time and searched until he found solid rock
to build his house on. But the other builder was
known as the foolish builder because he didn't
pay attention to the teaching and built his house
directly on the sand.

Shortly after both houses were finished, the
rain began to fall and the wind began to blow.
It rained so much that water surrounded both

houses, and the wind blew so hard that the houses began to shake.

Because the foolish builder's house was built right on top of the sand, his house broke apart and was washed away by the rain. But the wise builder's house stood strong all through the storm because he had obeyed what he was taught. He had built his house on a solid rock!

When Jesus finished telling this story, the people were amazed because they knew that God had sent Him to teach them to obey His lessons.

Pray with Me

Dear God, thank You for teaching me
Your lessons. Please help me learn
to live like You want me to so I can be
strong even in difficult times. Amen.

Take It with You . . .

When I listen to Jesus, I will
be like the wise builder
and stay strong when bad
things happen.

Ann White
In Grace Ministries, Marietta, GA

Week :: 33 ::

Lost and Found

LUKE 15:1–10

Many tax collectors and "sinners" came to listen to Jesus. The Pharisees and the teachers of the law began to complain: "Look! This man welcomes sinners and even eats with them!" Then Jesus told them this story: "Suppose one of you has 100 sheep, but he loses 1 of them. Then he will leave the other 99 sheep alone and go out and look for the lost sheep. The man will keep on searching for the lost sheep until he finds it. And when he finds it, the man is very happy. He puts it on his shoulders and goes home. He calls to his friends and neighbors and says, 'Be happy with me because I found my lost sheep!' In the same way, I tell you there is much joy in heaven when 1 sinner changes his heart. There is more joy for that 1 sinner than there is for 99 good people who don't need to change. Suppose a woman has

ten silver coins, but she loses one of them. She will light a lamp and clean the house. She will look carefully for the coin until she finds it. And when she finds it, she will call her friends and neighbors and say, 'Be happy with me because I have found the coin that I lost!' In the same way, there is joy before the angels of God when 1 sinner changes his heart."

TODAY'S ADVENTURE

Jesus is our Rescuer! He rescues people who are lost from Him because of sin. Jesus told stories about lost things that needed to be rescued. He did this to help people understand how He can be their Rescuer too.

Jesus told a story about a shepherd who had one hundred sheep. One day, when the shepherd counted his sheep, he realized he had only ninety-nine. Now, ninety-nine sheep are a *lot* of sheep, and the shepherd could have been happy. But the shepherd was *not* happy. Every single sheep was important to him. So he left the ninety-nine sheep and searched for the one that was missing.

When the shepherd found the lost sheep, he rescued it and carried it safely home. The shepherd celebrated with his family and friends. "Hooray!" he said to them. "I have rescued my lost sheep!"

Jesus told another story to the people about a woman who had ten silver coins. The coins were very important to her. One day, as she counted her coins, she realized she had only nine. Now, nine silver coins are a *lot* of silver coins, and she could have been happy. But the woman was *not* happy. Every coin mattered to *this* woman. So she turned on all the lights in her house and cleaned and searched until she found the coin. Then she called everyone to celebrate with her. "Hooray!" she said to everyone. "I have rescued my lost coin!"

Jesus said, "Each person who is lost from Me because of sin is important and matters to Me. When I rescue a person who is lost because of sin, all of heaven celebrates just like the people in the stories."

"Hooray!" we all say. "A lost friend has been saved!"

Pray with Me

Dear God, thank You for sending Jesus to be my Rescuer from sin and making a way for me never to be lost from You. Amen.

Take It with You . . .

Jesus loves me and will rescue me from sin when I ask Him to.

Analisa Hood and Suzanne Walker
Mobberly Baptist Church, Longview, TX

The Father Who Loves His Children

LUKE 15:11–24

Then Jesus said, "A man had two sons. The younger son said to his father, 'Give me my share of the property.' So the father divided the property between his two sons. Then the younger son gathered up all that was his and left. He traveled far away to another country. There he wasted his money in foolish living. He spent everything that he had. Soon after that, the land became very dry, and there was no rain. There was not enough food to eat anywhere in the country. The son was hungry and needed money. So he got a job with one of the citizens there. The man sent the son into the fields to feed pigs. The son was so hungry that he was willing to eat the food the pigs were eating. But no one gave him anything. The son realized that he had been very foolish. He thought, 'All of my father's servants have plenty of food. But I am here, almost dying with hunger. I will leave and return

to my father. I'll say to him: Father, I have sinned against God and against you. I am not good enough to be called your son. But let me be like one of your servants.' So the son left and went to his father. "While the son was still a long way off, his father saw him coming. He felt sorry for his son. So the father ran to him, and hugged and kissed him. The son said, 'Father, I have sinned against God and against you. I am not good enough to be called your son.' But the father said to his servants, 'Hurry! Bring the best clothes and put them on him. Also, put a ring on his finger and sandals on his feet. And get our fat calf and kill it. Then we can have a feast and celebrate! My son was dead, but now he is alive again! He was lost, but now he is found!' So they began to celebrate."

One day Jesus told a story about a good father who had two sons and a farm. The father loved his sons very much. But the younger son did not want to work for his father anymore. He knew that one day, he would receive part of his father's money, and he wanted it early. He wanted to leave the farm and go far away. He asked his father for the money, and the father gave it to him. The father was sad when his son left home and went far away.

While the son was gone, he did many wrong things. He even spent all his money, and when it was gone, he was hungry and worried. He was sorry he had done bad things, and he missed his father. He knew his father's servants had a better life than he did. He would go home and be a servant. So he started walking back. It took him a long time to walk so far.

While he was still walking, the father saw him coming and ran to meet him. The son told his father he was sorry for what he had done. The father loved his son so much and was so glad he had come home that he hugged and kissed him. The father even gave his son a big party and invited his friends to come and celebrate with him. His son had been lost, but now he was found!

Did you know God loves you the way the father in the story loved his son? God will always love you. Jesus wants you to tell God you are sorry when you do bad things. Jesus wants you to love God too. When you love God, it makes Jesus happy.

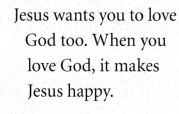

Pray with Me

Dear Lord, I am sorry when I do bad things. Thank You for loving me like a good father loves his children. Amen.

Take It with You . . .

God loves me. When I do wrong, I will tell Him I am sorry.

Dr. J. Kie Bowman
Hyde Park Baptist Church, Austin, TX

Love Your Neighbor

LUKE 10:25–37

hen a teacher of the law stood up. He was trying to test Jesus. He said, "Teacher, what must I do to get life forever?" Jesus said to him, "What is written in the law? What do you read there?" The man answered, "Love the Lord your God. Love him with all your heart, all your soul, all your strength, and all your mind." Also, "You must love your neighbor as you love yourself." Jesus said to him, "Your answer is right. Do this and you will have life forever." But the man wanted

to show that the way he was living was right.
So he said to Jesus, "And who is my neighbor?"
To answer this question, Jesus said, "A man
was going down the road from Jerusalem to
Jericho. Some robbers attacked him. They
tore off his clothes and beat him. Then they
left him lying there, almost dead. It happened
that a Jewish priest was going down that road.
When the priest saw the man,
he walked by on the other
side of the road. Next,
a Levite came there.

He went over and looked at the man. Then he walked by on the other side of the road. Then a Samaritan traveling down the road came to where the hurt man was lying. He saw the man and felt very sorry for him. The Samaritan went to him and poured olive oil and wine on his wounds and bandaged them. He put the hurt man on his own donkey and took him to an inn. At the inn, the Samaritan took care of him. The next day, the Samaritan brought out two silver coins and gave them to the innkeeper. The Samaritan said, 'Take care of this man. If you spend more money on him, I will pay it back to you when I come again.'" Then Jesus said, "Which one of these three men do you think was a neighbor to the man who was attacked by the robbers?" The teacher of the law answered, "The one who helped him." Jesus said to him, "Then go and do the same thing he did!"

TODAY'S ADVENTURE

In the Bible, Jesus tells us to love the Lord our God and to love our neighbor. Who is *your* neighbor?

Your neighbor can be anyone. It might be someone in your neighborhood or at your school, but it can also be someone you do not know. What do you think God would want you to do if you saw someone fall down on the playground? God would want you to help that person up!

Jesus told a story about a man who was walking down the road when some really bad men attacked him and took everything he had. They even tore his clothes! They left him on the side of the road. He was hurt and could not get up.

Later, a priest walked by and saw the hurt man. He decided to walk on the other side of the road. He did not even try to help the hurt man.

Then a Levite walked by and saw the man on the ground. He also decided to walk by on the other side of the road. He did not try to help him either.

Finally, a Samaritan saw the man on the ground. He quickly ran to him and began to help him. He cleaned and bandaged all of his hurts. He picked him up and put him on his donkey. The Samaritan knew the injured man needed a place to rest. He took him to an inn, which was like a hotel. He gave the innkeeper two silver coins to take care of the injured man.

Which of these three men do you think loved his neighbor? The priest, the Levite, or the Samaritan? The Samaritan showed love to his neighbor by helping him. Follow the example of the Samaritan and show God's love to everyone!

Pray with Me

Dear Lord, help me be a good neighbor to my friends and even to the people I do not know. When they need help, let me be like the Samaritan and help them. Amen.

Take It with You . . .

Jesus says I should love my neighbor as myself.

Mary Cox
North Metro Baptist Church, Lawrenceville, GA

Helping Your Friend Have Faith

MARK 2:1–11

A few days later, Jesus came back to Capernaum. The news spread that he was home. So many people gathered to hear him preach that the house was full. There was no place to stand, not even outside the door. Jesus was teaching them. Some people came, bringing a paralyzed man to Jesus. Four of them were carrying the paralyzed man. But they could not get to Jesus because of the crowd. So they went to the roof above Jesus and made a hole in the roof. Then they lowered the mat with the paralyzed man on it. Jesus saw that these men had great faith. So he said to the paralyzed man, "Young man, your sins are forgiven." Some of the teachers of the law were sitting there. They saw what Jesus did, and they said to themselves, "Why does this man say things like that? He is saying

things that are against God. Only God can forgive sins." At once Jesus knew what these teachers of the law were thinking. So he said to them, "Why are you thinking these things? Which is easier: to tell this paralyzed man, 'Your sins are forgiven,' or to tell him, 'Stand up. Take your mat and walk'? But I will prove to you that the Son of Man has authority on earth to forgive sins." So Jesus said to the paralyzed man, "I tell you, stand up. Take your mat and go home."

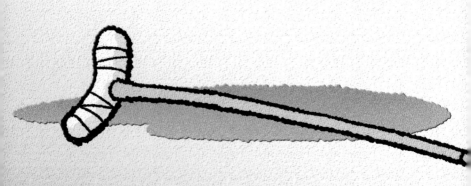

When the people heard that Jesus was teaching in a house in Capernaum, they were excited and hurried to hear Him. Four men wanted very much to help their friend, who could not walk. They took him to see Jesus, but the house was too crowded for them to get inside. So they picked up their friend and carried him up onto the roof of the house. Then they cut a hole in the roof and lowered their friend down into the room where Jesus was teaching.

When Jesus saw what these men had done for their friend, He told the man who could not walk that his sins were forgiven. Then Jesus told him to stand up because he was now healed. The man stood up and walked out of the house! Jesus helped the man walk because his friends had faith. Meeting Jesus changed the man's life.

All this happened because four men wanted to help their friend meet Jesus, and they did not give up. Will you help your friends meet Jesus? When you invite your friends to church, you can help them to have faith in Him.

Do not give up! Bring your friends to Jesus! When you do, Jesus will help them.

Pray with Me

Dear God, I want to bring my friends to Jesus and help them have faith. Please help me bring them to Jesus without giving up. Amen.

Take It with You . . .

I will bring a friend to Jesus this week. I will invite someone to come to church with me.

Dr. Ronnie Floyd
Cross Church, Northwest Arkansas

A Surprising Lunch

MARK 6:30–44

The apostles that Jesus had sent out to preach returned. They gathered around him and told him about all the things they had done and taught. Crowds of people were coming and going. Jesus and his followers did not even have time to eat. He said to them, "Come with me. We will go to a quiet place to be alone. There we will get some rest." So they went in a boat alone to a place where there were no people. But many people saw them leave and recognized them. So people from all the towns ran to the place where

Jesus was going. They got there before Jesus arrived. When he landed, he saw a great crowd waiting. Jesus felt sorry for them, because they were like sheep without a shepherd. So he taught them many things. It was now late in the day. Jesus' followers came to him and said, "No one lives in this place. And it is already very late. Send the people away. They need to go to the farms and towns around here to buy

some food to eat." But Jesus answered, "You give them food to eat." They said to him, "We can't buy enough bread to feed all these people! We would all have to work a month to earn enough money to buy that much bread!" Jesus asked them, "How many loaves of bread do you have now? Go and see." When they found out, they came to him and said, "We have five loaves and two fish." Then Jesus said to the followers, "Tell all the people to sit in groups on the green grass." So all the people sat in groups. They sat in groups of 50 or groups of 100. Jesus took the five loaves and two fish. He looked up to heaven and thanked God for the bread. He divided the bread and gave it to his followers for them to give to the people. Then he divided the two fish among them all. All the people ate and were satisfied. The followers filled 12 baskets with the pieces of bread and fish that were not eaten. There were about 5,000 men there who ate.

One day Jesus decided He wanted to spend time
with just His best friends. So they got in a boat
and traveled across the lake.

A crowd of people saw Jesus leaving. They
wanted to be with Jesus, so they hurried on foot to
the other side of the lake and arrived before Jesus.
When Jesus saw the people, He felt sorry for them
because they were like sheep without a shepherd.
He decided to spend time with them.

After a while, Jesus' friends saw that it was
getting late and the people were hungry. There
was nowhere to get anything to eat. Jesus' friends
told Jesus to send the people into the nearby
towns and get some food to eat.

But Jesus told *them* to feed the people. They
were surprised. There were more than five
thousand people there! The only food they had

was two small fish and five loaves of bread. The friends knew that would not feed everyone.

Jesus told the people to sit down on the grass. He took the bread and fish, looked up to heaven, and blessed the food. He divided the fish and bread into pieces and gave it to His friends to hand out.

All the people ate and ate. They ate until they were full. Then Jesus told His friends to pick up the food that was left over. They picked up twelve baskets of food!

Jesus' friends were amazed. When Jesus asked them to feed the people, they looked at what they *did not have*. But Jesus looked at what they *did have* and then looked to God. The Bible tells us that with God all things are possible.

When you are faced with something you think you can't do, look at what you have, look to God, and ask God to bless it. You may be surprised by what happens.

Pray with Me

Dear God, thank You for teaching me what to do when I have something really hard to do. Amen.

Take It with You . . .

When faced with tough things to do, I will ask God to bless what I have.

Anne Chenault
First Baptist Church, Chipley, FL

Walking on Water with Jesus

MATTHEW 14:22–36

Then Jesus made his followers get into the boat. He told them to go ahead of him to the other side of the lake. Jesus stayed there to tell the people they could go home. After he said good-bye to them, he went alone up into the hills to pray. It was late, and Jesus was there alone. By this time, the boat was already far away on the lake. The boat was having trouble because of the waves, and the wind was blowing against it. Between three and six o'clock in the morning,

Jesus' followers were still in the boat. Jesus came to them. He was walking on the water. When the followers saw him walking on the water, they were afraid. They said, "It's a ghost!" and cried out in fear. But Jesus quickly spoke to them. He said, "Have courage! It is I! Don't be afraid." Peter said, "Lord, if that is really you, then tell me to come to you on the water." Jesus said, "Come." And Peter left the boat and walked on the water to Jesus. But when

Peter saw the wind and the waves, he became afraid and began to sink. He shouted, "Lord, save me!" Then Jesus reached out his hand and caught Peter. Jesus said, "Your faith is small. Why did you doubt?" After Peter and Jesus were in the boat, the wind became calm. Then those who were in the boat worshiped Jesus and said, "Truly you are the Son of God!" After they crossed the lake, they came to the shore at Gennesaret. The people there saw Jesus and knew who he was. So they told people all around there that Jesus had come. They brought all their sick to him. They begged Jesus to let them just touch the edge of his coat to be healed. And all the sick people who touched it were healed.

Jesus will always save us if we believe in Him and look for Him when we are afraid.

Jesus and His friends had spent the day along the shore of a lake, helping people who were hungry. When He was done, Jesus told His friends to go to the other side of the lake in a boat. After they left, Jesus went into the hills to pray.

Jesus' friends had gone far out onto the lake when the wind started blowing. This made the waves grow bigger, and the boat was rocking back and forth.

In the middle of the night, Jesus began to walk on the water toward the boat. This scared His friends. They did not know it was Jesus, and they shouted, "It is a ghost!"

Right away, Jesus told them not to be afraid because He was the one coming to them. One of

Jesus' friends was named Peter. Peter asked Jesus to invite him to come out on the water with Him. So Jesus told Peter to come to Him.

Peter got out of the boat and began to walk on the water too! But when he felt the wind and saw the waves, he became very scared. Peter began to sink into the water. He yelled, "Lord, save me!" Jesus reached out His hand and caught Peter. He asked Peter why he did not believe.

After that, they both climbed into the boat and the wind became calm. All the other friends were very excited about what Jesus had done, and they all agreed that He was the true Son of God.

They all went to the shore, and Jesus helped many sick people.

When you are afraid, pray to Jesus. He is with you and will help you be brave. He is always there to rescue you!

Pray with Me

Dear God, thank You for watching over me. I know that if I trust in Jesus, I do not ever need to be afraid. Amen.

Take It with You . . .

I must always look to Jesus to help me when I am afraid.

Mary Eppl
First Baptist Orlando, Orlando, FL

Who's Afraid of the Big Bad Storm?

MARK 4:35–41

That evening, Jesus said to his followers, "Come with me across the lake." He and the followers left the people there. They went in the boat that Jesus was already sitting in. There were also other boats with them. A very strong wind came up on the lake. The waves began coming over the sides and into the boat. It was almost full of water. Jesus was at the back of the boat, sleeping with his head on a pillow. The followers went to him and woke him. They said, "Teacher, do you care about us? We will drown!" Jesus stood up and commanded the wind and the waves to stop. He said, "Quiet! Be still!" Then the wind stopped, and the lake became calm. Jesus said to his followers, "Why are you afraid? Do you still have no faith?" The followers were very afraid and asked each other, "What kind of man is this? Even the wind and the waves obey him!"

Have you ever been afraid? What did you do? One evening, Jesus' disciples were very afraid. Jesus and His disciples had been teaching when He said to them, "Let's cross to the other side of the lake." His disciples then got into Jesus' boat and they, along with other boats, started across the lake.

All of a sudden the wind began to howl, and the waves started to get higher and higher until they were crashing over the boat. The disciples started to panic because the water was filling the boat.

Where was Jesus during all of this? Did He know what was happening? The disciples looked over at Jesus and saw that He was asleep! They could not believe this and said, "Teacher, do you not care that we are going to drown?"

Jesus stood up in the middle of the storm and said, "Quiet, be still." The wind and the waves obeyed Jesus, and everything was calm. Jesus then looked at His disciples and said, "Why are you afraid? Do you not have any faith?" The disciples were afraid. They could not believe that the wind and waves had obeyed Jesus!

Jesus is always there for you, and He will never leave you. During the scary times, remember that He is in control of everything, even a storm. Have faith and believe that Jesus is who He says He is.

Dear God, I am so glad that You are always there for me. Help me have faith in You and learn to trust You even in the scary times. Amen.

Take It with You . . .

Jesus wants me to remember that He is in control of all things.

Dr. D'Ann Laywell
North Richland Hills Baptist Church, North Richland Hills, TX

Choose to Enjoy Jesus

LUKE 10:38–42

While Jesus and his followers were traveling, Jesus went into a town. A woman named Martha let Jesus stay at her house. Martha had a sister named Mary. Mary was sitting at Jesus' feet and listening to him teach. Martha became angry because she had so much work to do. She went in and said, "Lord, don't you care that my sister has left me alone to do all the work? Tell her to help me!" But the Lord answered her, "Martha, Martha, you are getting worried and upset about too many things. Only one thing is important. Mary has chosen the right thing, and it will never be taken away from her."

In this story we get to see Jesus doing what He loves most—being with people.

Jesus was invited to come over to His friends' house for dinner. One of His friends, Martha, was busy working while Jesus was there. Her sister, Mary, spent her time sitting with Jesus and listening to Him.

Martha felt upset because she thought her sister should be helping her cook the food and clean the house. She wanted Jesus to make Mary help her. But Jesus said that Mary was doing the right thing by being with Him. It is easy to be busy, but Jesus sometimes wants us to just enjoy being with Him, rather than being too busy to spend time with Him.

You probably have a best friend. You like to be with that person and play together and talk together. Friends spend time with each other. Jesus is waiting for you to spend time with Him too. He's the best Friend you will ever have.

Pray with Me

Dear Lord, You're the best friend I have. You are always there with me. I want to know You more, and I'm excited to spend time with You. Amen.

Take It with You . . .

I will thank God for allowing me to spend time with Him.

Hollie Hixson
Cross Point Church, Nashville, TN

Week :: 41 ::

Believing in Jesus

JOHN 11:23, 25–29, 32–34, 41–44

Jesus said, "Your brother will rise and live again." . . . Jesus said to her, "I am the resurrection and the life. He who believes in me will have life even if he dies. And he who lives and believes in me will never die. Martha, do you believe this?" Martha answered, "Yes, Lord. I believe that you are the Christ, the Son of God. You are the One who was coming to the world." After Martha said this, she went back to her sister Mary. She talked to Mary alone. Martha said, "The Teacher is here and he is asking for you." When Mary heard this, she got up quickly and went to Jesus. . . . But Mary went to the place where Jesus was. When she saw him, she fell at his feet and said, "Lord, if you had been here, my brother would not have died." Jesus saw that Mary was crying and that the Jews who came with her were crying, too. Jesus felt very sad in his heart and was deeply troubled.

He asked, "Where did you bury him?" "Come and see, Lord," they said. . . . So they moved the stone away from the entrance. Then Jesus looked up and said, "Father, I thank you that you heard me. I know that you always hear me. But I said these things because of the people here around me. I want them to believe that you sent me." After Jesus said this, he cried out in a loud voice, "Lazarus, come out!" The dead man came out. His hands and feet were wrapped with pieces of cloth, and he had a cloth around his face. Jesus said to them, "Take the cloth off of him and let him go."

Jesus showed His power by bringing His friend Lazarus back to life. Lazarus came out of the grave, proving that nothing, not even death, can stop Jesus. The Bible tells us we have nothing to fear when we believe in Jesus and we are His friend. We have His promise that we will live with Him forever in heaven, and He always keeps His promises.

The story of Lazarus is also about his sisters, Mary and Martha. They believed in Jesus. They knew that if He had come sooner, their brother, Lazarus, would not have died.

Yes, Jesus could have come sooner and healed him, but Jesus wanted to do more than heal Lazarus from sickness. Jesus wanted to raise His friend from the dead so that many more people would believe in Him.

Like Mary and Martha, you can ask Jesus for help. Sometimes it may seem that He does not want to answer your prayers. This is not because He does not love you or cannot do it. It may be that Jesus wants to do something even greater and more amazing than what you asked Him to do.

Learn to be patient and trust in Jesus, even when it is hard. You can trust Jesus because He always knows what to do, and He will always do what is best.

Pray with Me

Dear Lord, I am happy to be Your friend. You always want what is best for me. Help me be patient and always trust in You. Amen.

Take It with You . . .

Jesus is my friend, and I believe in Him. He cares for me and will do what is best for me.

Dr. David Fleming
Champion Forest Baptist Church, Houston, TX

Jesus Changes Everything!

LUKE 19:1–10

Jesus was going through the city of Jericho. In Jericho there was a man named Zacchaeus. He was a wealthy, very important tax collector. He wanted to see who Jesus was, but he was too short to see above the crowd. He ran ahead to a place where he knew Jesus would come. He climbed a sycamore tree so he could see Jesus. When Jesus came to that place, he looked up and saw Zacchaeus in the tree. He said to him, "Zacchaeus, hurry and come down! I must stay at your house today." Zacchaeus came down quickly. He was pleased to have Jesus in his house. All the people saw this and began to complain, "Look at the kind of man Jesus stays with. Zacchaeus is a sinner!" But Zacchaeus said to

the Lord, "I will give half of my money to the poor. If I have cheated anyone, I will pay that person back four times more!" Jesus said, "Salvation has come to this house today. This man truly belongs to the family of Abraham. The Son of Man came to find lost people and save them."

One day Jesus was walking through town.
Zacchaeus had heard about Jesus, and now he
wanted to see Him. But Zacchaeus was too short.
He could not see through the crowd or over the
tops of their heads. So he climbed up into the top
of a sycamore tree.

Jesus saw him and said, "Come down,
Zacchaeus. I want to stay at your house today!"
Could it really be that Jesus was going to
Zacchaeus's house? Why would Jesus spend time
with a person like this? Even though Zacchaeus
had done some bad things, Jesus loved him and
wanted to get to know him.

Once Zacchaeus met Jesus, his life changed! Instead of stealing from other people, Zacchaeus decided to give half of his money away to the poor people. He also promised to give any money back that he had stolen. In fact, he promised to give back four times the amount he stole!

Talk to Jesus today. When you spend time with Him, He will change you to be more like Him.

Pray with Me

Dear God, help me be a changed person because of Jesus. Help me love people like You do. Amen.

Take It with You . . .

Meeting Jesus changes everything.

Pastor Kelly Bullard
Temple Baptist Church, Fayetteville, NC

Amazing
Healing

JOHN 9:1–3, 6–7, 13–15

As Jesus was walking along, he saw a man who had been born blind. His followers asked him, "Teacher, whose sin caused this man to be born blind—his own sin or his parents' sin?" Jesus answered, "It is not this man's sin or his parents' sin that made him blind. This man was born blind so that God's power could be shown in him." . . . After Jesus said this, he spit on

the ground and made some mud with it. He put the mud on the man's eyes. Then he told the man, "Go and wash in the Pool of Siloam." (Siloam means Sent.) So the man went to the pool. He washed and came back. And he was able to see. . . . Then the people took to the Pharisees the man who had been blind. The day Jesus had made mud and healed his eyes was a Sabbath day. So now the Pharisees asked the man, "How did you get your sight?" He answered, "He put mud on my eyes. I washed, and now I can see."

The man Jesus met in this story was born blind. He never saw the blue sky, the green grass, his parents' faces, or what his house looked like. His parents had probably taken him to see a lot of doctors. They might have tried every medicine they could find, or prayed every night that their son would be able to see. But the man still could not see.

One day the man met someone who would change everything, and His name was Jesus. Jesus healed the blind man so that he could see! Can you imagine how amazing that must have been to see color or his best friend's face, or to watch the sun set for the first time? The fact that Jesus healed the blind man is awesome enough, but what is even more awesome is how Jesus chose to do it!

Jesus could have waved His hand or snapped His fingers, and the man would have been able to see. Jesus is God, and He can heal anything. But what did Jesus do? He spit in the dirt, made mud, and rubbed the mud in the man's eyes!

Jesus can do amazing, awesome things that we can only dream of, and a lot of times He uses the most unlikely objects and people to do them. If Jesus can heal a blind man with some spit and dirt, imagine how He could use you.

Dear God, thank You for the amazing healing You have done for others and for me. Amen.

Take It with You . . .

God can perform amazing works with unlikely people, and that includes me!

Ryan Hartzell
The Creek Church, London, KY

Jesus'
Last Meal

MARK 14:17–26

In the evening, Jesus went to that house with the 12. While they were all eating, Jesus said, "I tell you the truth. One of you will give me to my enemies—one of you eating with me now." The followers were very sad to hear this. Each one said to Jesus, "I am not the one, am I?" Jesus answered, "The man who is against me is 1 of the 12. He is the 1 who dips his bread into the bowl with me. The Son of

Man must go and die. The Scriptures say
this will happen. But how terrible it will be
for the person who gives the Son of Man to
be killed. It would be better for that person
if he had never been born." While they were
eating, Jesus took some bread. He thanked
God for it and broke it. Then he gave it to his
followers and said, "Take it. This bread is my
body." Then Jesus took a cup. He thanked
God for it and gave it
to the followers.

All the followers drank from the cup. Then Jesus said, "This is my blood which begins the new agreement that God makes with his people. This blood is poured out for many. I tell you the truth. I will not drink of this fruit of the vine again until that day when I drink it new in the kingdom of God." They sang a hymn and went out to the Mount of Olives.

What is your favorite type of food? Do you like pizza or macaroni and cheese? Jesus liked to eat too. When He was on earth, He often ate fish (John 6:9 and 21:9). He also ate a lot of bread.

The night before Jesus died, He had a meal with His best friends. Do you know what they ate? Bread and a special drink. But this was not a normal meal. Jesus used the food to teach a lesson.

He held up His bread and said, "This bread is like My body." Bread was different in Jesus' world. It wasn't like the fluffy loaves that come from the grocery store today. It was thin, easy to break, and had little toasty holes all over it.

Jesus wanted His friends to know that His body was going to be like that bread. So that Jesus could pay for our sins, His body was going to be broken and bruised on a cross.

After eating the bread, Jesus gave His friends something to drink, and He said, "My blood will wash your hearts clean of sins."

Jesus knew He would sacrifice Himself for our sins. His blood washes away all of our sins. When you trust Jesus to forgive you of all of the bad things you have done, He will get rid of all the dirty sin in your heart and make your heart clean.

Pray with Me

Dear God, thank You for loving me.
Thank You that Jesus died for my sins!
Help me love You and live for You.
Amen.

Take It with You . . .

Next time I thank God for
my food, I will also thank
Him for Jesus.

Dr. Patrick Latham
First Baptist Church Lawton-Fort Sill, Lawton, OK

Who Is Jesus?

MATTHEW 21:1–14

Jesus and his followers were coming closer to Jerusalem. But first they stopped at Bethphage at the hill called the Mount of Olives. From there Jesus sent two of his followers into the town. He said to them, "Go to the town you can see there. When you enter it, you will find a donkey tied there with its colt. Untie them and bring them to me. If anyone asks you why you are taking the donkeys, tell him, 'The Master needs them. He will send them back soon.'" This was to make clear the full meaning of what the prophet said:

"Tell the people of Jerusalem,
  'Your king is coming to you.
He is gentle and riding on a donkey.
  He is on the colt of a donkey.'"

The followers went and did what Jesus told
them to do. They brought the donkey and the
colt to Jesus.
They laid
their
coats
on the
donkeys,
and Jesus
sat on them.
Many people
spread their
coats on the road
before Jesus.

Others cut branches from the trees and spread them on the road. Some of the people were walking ahead of Jesus. Others were walking behind him. All the people were shouting,

> "Praise to the Son of David!
> God bless the One who comes in the
>   name of the Lord!
> Praise to God in heaven!"

Then Jesus went into Jerusalem. The city was filled with excitement. The people asked, "Who is this man?" The crowd answered, "This man is Jesus. He is the prophet from the town of Nazareth in Galilee." Jesus went into the Temple. He threw out all the people who were buying and selling there. He turned over the tables that belonged to the men who were exchanging different kinds of money. And he upset the benches of those who were selling doves. Jesus said to all the people there, "It is written in the Scriptures, 'My Temple will be a house where people will pray.' But you are changing God's house into a 'hideout for robbers.'" The blind and crippled people came to Jesus in the Temple, and Jesus healed them.

TODAY'S ADVENTURE

Many years before Jesus came to earth, men called prophets spoke God's words and gave clues so that people would be able to recognize Jesus when He came. One of the clues they gave was that Jesus, their King, would ride into Jerusalem on a donkey instead of on a horse. This would be different from what any other king before Jesus had done.

When Jesus was walking to Jerusalem, He sent two of His followers into the town to look for a donkey. They came back with the animal, and Jesus rode it into Jerusalem. The people were so excited to see Jesus! They walked along with Him and put branches on the road in front of Him. As He rode along, they were shouting about His greatness and that He came from God.

Even though Jesus riding on a donkey into Jerusalem was a clue given many years before, most of the people still didn't understand who Jesus was and asked, "Who is this man?" They thought He was just a man who spoke God's words.

After entering the temple where people prayed to God, Jesus became upset. He saw men selling animals for money, so He turned over their tables. He said that the temple was made to be a place where people prayed to God and learned about His goodness, not a place for making money.

Then Jesus began to heal people who were blind and had other sicknesses. By healing people, Jesus was helping everyone see that He was the Son of God and that He came to love and care for people.

Pray with Me

Dear God, help us know who You are and why You came so that we can tell others about You. Amen.

Take It with You . . .

Jesus came to love and care for all people.

Norma Bowers
Flint-Groves Baptist Church, Gastonia, NC

The Garden

LUKE 22:39–53

Jesus left the city and went to the Mount of Olives. His followers went with him. (Jesus went there often.) He said to his followers, "Pray for strength against temptation." Then Jesus went about a stone's throw away from them. He kneeled down and prayed, "Father, if it is what you want, then let me not have this cup of suffering. But do what you want, not what I want." Then an angel from heaven appeared to him to help him. Jesus was full of pain; he prayed even more.

Sweat dripped from his face as if he were bleeding. When he finished praying, he went to his followers. They were asleep. (Their sadness had made them very tired.) Jesus said to them, "Why are you sleeping? Get up and pray for strength against temptation." While Jesus was speaking, a crowd came up. One of the 12 apostles was leading them. He was Judas. He came close to Jesus so that he could kiss him.
But Jesus said to him, "Judas, are

you using the kiss to give the Son of Man to his enemies?" The followers of Jesus were standing there too. They saw what was happening. They said to Jesus, "Lord, should we use our swords?" And one of them did use his sword. He cut off the right ear of the servant of the high priest. Jesus said, "Stop!" Then he touched the servant's ear and healed him. Those who came to arrest Jesus were the leading priests, the soldiers who guarded the Temple, and the Jewish elders. Jesus said to them, "Why did you come out here with swords and sticks? Do you think I am a criminal? I was with you every day in the Temple. Why didn't you try to arrest me there? But this is your time—the time when darkness rules."

After a busy week in Jerusalem, Jesus went to pray in a place called the garden of Gethsemane. Jesus spent time talking to God. He was upset because He knew that soon He would have to leave His friends. He prayed to God while His friends, who were supposed to be praying, fell asleep in the Garden.

Jesus was waking them up when Judas—one of the twelve men Jesus spent most of His time with—arrived with a group of soldiers who had come to arrest Jesus. Peter and Jesus' other friends became angry and wanted to fight with the soldiers. Peter even cut off one of the soldier's ears! Jesus did not want the group to fight. He touched the soldier's ear, and the soldier was all better. Jesus wanted to show that we should love even those who do not show love toward us.

It is hard to believe that Jesus would be so kind to someone who was there to be so mean to Him. Jesus taught His friends and us two major things while He was in the garden. He taught us that we are supposed to pray to God when we are upset and need help. He also taught us that we should love all people, even if they are not nice to us.

Follow Jesus' example and ask God for help when you are hurt or scared. Love both your friends *and* the people who aren't kind to you. God is always happy when you try to be more like Jesus.

Pray with Me

Dear God, thank You for listening to me when I am upset. Help me love all people because You love all people. Amen.

Take It with You . . .

I will try hard to love all people.

Rev. David Richardson
First Baptist Church, Creedmoor, NC

Jesus Went Through Pain for a Purpose

JOHN 19:16–24

S o Pilate gave Jesus to them to be killed on a cross. The soldiers took charge of Jesus. Carrying his own cross, Jesus went out to a place called The Place of the Skull. (In the Jewish language this place is called Golgotha.) There they nailed Jesus to the cross. They also put two other men on crosses, one on each side of Jesus with Jesus in the middle. Pilate wrote a sign and put it on the cross. It read: "JESUS OF NAZARETH, THE KING OF THE JEWS." The sign was written in the Jewish language, in Latin, and in Greek. Many of the Jews read the sign, because this place where Jesus was killed was near the city. The leading Jewish priests said to Pilate, "Don't write, 'The King of the Jews.' But write, 'This man said, I am the King of the Jews.'" Pilate answered, "What I have written, I have written!" After the soldiers nailed Jesus to the cross, they took his clothes. They divided them into four parts. Each soldier got one

part. They also took his long shirt. It was all one piece of cloth, woven from top to bottom. So the soldiers said to each other, "We should not tear this into parts. We should throw lots to see who will get it." This happened to give full meaning to the Scripture:

> "They divided my clothes among them.
> And they threw lots for my clothing."

So the soldiers did this.

Everybody gets hurt once in a while. You have probably fallen down, scraped your knee, or pinched your finger, and you know that hurts. That kind of hurt is called physical pain. But did you know that there are other types of pain? When someone is mean to you and you get your feelings hurt, that is pain too. When you are lonely or scared, that is pain, as well.

Jesus knows about pain. On the cross, Jesus was hurt in every way you have been hurt, and even worse. He was in pain from the nails that were put in His hands and feet. His feelings were hurt by the soldiers who were mean to Him and took His clothes. He felt lonely because His friends were scared and ran away. Jesus knows all about pain.

But there is something very special about the pain of Jesus. You probably do everything you can to avoid pain by wearing a helmet, being careful, and staying close to your family. But Jesus did not run away from pain. He volunteered to go through it. Can you believe that? Jesus chose to die on the cross. Jesus allowed the soldiers to take His clothes. Jesus knew that His friends would run away. Why would He choose to go through all that pain? Because Jesus loves you.

When Jesus died on the cross, He was taking the punishment that you should have received for your sins. The Bible says in 1 Peter 3:18, "Christ himself died for you. And that one death paid for your sins. He was not guilty, but he died for those who are guilty. He did this to bring you all to God. His body was killed, but he was made alive in the spirit." Thank Jesus for His amazing love.

Pray with Me

Dear God, I'm so sorry that Jesus went through so much pain on the cross for my sins. I want to be Your friend and follow You forever! Amen.

Take It with You . . .

I will tell everyone I know that Jesus died for me!

Pastor John Welborn
Crosslink Community Church, Harrisonburg, VA

Jesus Is Missing

MATTHEW 28:1–4; JOHN 20:1–10

The day after the Sabbath day was the first day of the week. At dawn on the first day, Mary Magdalene and another woman named Mary went to look at the tomb. At that time there was a strong earthquake. An angel of the Lord came down from heaven. The angel went to the tomb and rolled the stone away from the entrance. Then he sat on the stone. He was shining as bright as lightning. His clothes were white as snow. The soldiers guarding the tomb were very frightened of the angel. They shook with fear and then became like dead men. . . .

Early on the first day of the week, Mary Magdalene went to the tomb. It was still dark. Mary saw that the large stone had been moved away from the tomb. So Mary ran to Simon Peter and the other follower (the one

Jesus loved). Mary said, "They have taken the Lord out of the tomb. We don't know where they have put him." So Peter and the other follower started for the tomb. They were both running, but the other follower ran faster than Peter. So the other follower reached the tomb first. He bent down and looked in. He saw the strips of linen cloth lying there, but he did not go in. Then following him came Simon Peter. He went into the tomb and saw the strips of linen lying there. He also saw the cloth that had been around Jesus' head. The cloth was folded up and laid in a different place from the strips of linen. Then the other follower, who had reached the tomb first, also went in. He saw and believed. (These followers did not yet understand from the Scriptures that Jesus must rise from death.) Then the followers went back home.

The Sunday morning after Jesus died, two ladies, both named Mary, went to the place where Jesus was buried. It was early in the morning, and it was still dark.

The ground shook, and an angel came down from heaven. The angel rolled away the large stone that covered the door of Jesus' tomb. The angel, who was dressed all in white and was very shiny, sat on the stone. The guards who had been watching the tomb were so scared they could not do anything.

One of the women saw that the tomb was empty. She ran and told Peter and John who were followers of Jesus that Jesus' body was not in the tomb. She thought someone had taken Him away. Peter and John ran to see for themselves.

Peter went into the tomb to look, but John only looked into the tomb and then waited outside. Jesus was not there, but the cloths He had been wrapped in when He was buried were still there. One piece was even folded neatly and lying by itself.

John decided to go in and look too. He saw the same thing Peter did. Then he believed that Jesus had risen up from being dead and had left the grave. Jesus' followers did not yet understand everything that had happened. But soon they would!

Jesus died and then rose from the dead for you and for all of us. He loves us that much! He loves *you* that much!

Pray with Me

Dear God, thank You for raising Jesus from being dead. Help me believe just as Your followers did. Amen.

Take It with You . . .

Even though Jesus died, He came back to life and is still alive today.

Dr. Phil Thomas
Shiloh Baptist Church, Fort Gaines, GA

Phillip Tells the Good News About Jesus

ACTS 8:26–33, 35–39

An angel of the Lord spoke to Philip. The angel said, "Get ready and go south. Go to the road that leads down to Gaza from Jerusalem—the desert road." So Philip got ready and went. On the road he saw a man from Ethiopia, a eunuch. He was an important officer in the service of Candace, the queen of the Ethiopians. He was responsible for taking care of all her money. He had gone to Jerusalem to worship, and now he was on his way home. He was sitting in his chariot and reading from the book of Isaiah, the prophet. The Spirit said to Philip,

"Go to that chariot and stay near it." So Philip
ran toward the chariot. He heard the man
reading from Isaiah, the prophet. Philip asked,
"Do you understand what you are reading?"
He answered, "How can I understand? I need
someone to explain it to me!" Then he invited
Philip to climb in and sit with him. The verse of
Scripture that he was reading was this:

"He was like a sheep being
led to be killed.
He was quiet, as a
sheep is quiet while
its wool is
being cut.

He said nothing.
    He was shamed and was treated
        unfairly.
    He died without children to continue his
        family.
    His life on earth has ended." . . .

Philip began to speak. He started with this same Scripture and told the man the Good News about Jesus. While they were traveling down the road, they came to some water. The officer said, "Look! Here is water! What is stopping me from being baptized?" [Philip answered, "If you believe with all your heart, you can." The officer said, "I believe that Jesus Christ is the Son of God."] Then the officer commanded the chariot to stop. Both Philip and the officer went down into the water, and Philip baptized him. When they came up out of the water, the Spirit of the Lord took Philip away; the officer never saw him again. The officer continued on his way home, full of joy.

Philip was a man who loved God. He wanted to tell everyone he met about God and the good news about Jesus.

One day an angel spoke to Philip and told him to travel down a certain road. The road was in the desert, so it was probably hot, rocky, and hard to walk, but Philip knew God wanted him to go, so he started walking.

Before long, he saw a man sitting in a chariot reading something. The Lord told Philip to get closer to the man. Philip obeyed and heard what the man was reading. He was excited when he realized the man was reading from God's Word. Now this man was from the land of Ethiopia, and he worked for the queen of Ethiopia. He was an important man who had a very important job.

Philip asked the man, "Do you understand what you are reading?" He answered, "No. Would you help me understand?"

So they traveled down the road in the chariot, and Philip told the man how God loved the people of the world so much that He sent His one and only Son, Jesus, to die for their sins so that they could live with Him in heaven forever.

When the Ethiopian heard the good news of Jesus, he stopped the chariot, looked at Philip, and said, "I believe that Jesus Christ is the Son of God! I want to be baptized." There was some water nearby, so both of them went down into the water. Philip baptized the Ethiopian!

After the man was baptized, God took Philip away to continue preaching and teaching other people about Him. The Ethiopian went home, rejoicing all the way because God had blessed him.

Pray with Me

Dear God, thank You for sending Jesus to us. I believe that Jesus is Your Son. Help me be brave and tell others the good news about Jesus. Amen.

Take It with You . . .

God loved me so much that He sent His Son to pay for my sins so that I may live in heaven with Him.

Judy Lee
There's Hope America Ministries, Cumming, GA

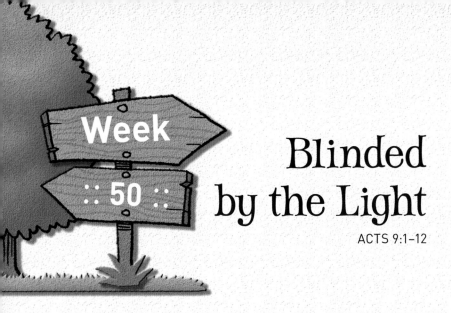

Blinded by the Light

ACTS 9:1–12

In Jerusalem Saul was still trying to frighten the followers of the Lord by saying he would kill them. So he went to the high priest and asked him to write letters to the synagogues in the city of Damascus. Saul wanted the high priest to give him the authority to find people in Damascus who were followers of Christ's Way. If he found any there, men or women, he would arrest them and bring them back to Jerusalem. So Saul went to Damascus. As he came near the city, a bright light from heaven suddenly flashed around him. Saul fell to the ground. He heard a voice saying to him, "Saul, Saul! Why are you doing things against me?" Saul said, "Who are you, Lord?" The voice answered, "I am Jesus. I am the One you are trying to hurt. Get up now and go into the city. Someone there will tell you what you must do." The men traveling with

Saul stood there, but they said nothing. They heard the voice, but they saw no one. Saul got up from the ground. He opened his eyes, but he could not see. So the men with Saul took his hand and led him into Damascus. For three days Saul could not see, and he did not eat or drink. There was a follower of Jesus in Damascus named Ananias. The Lord spoke to Ananias in a vision, "Ananias!" Ananias answered, "Here I am, Lord." The Lord said to him, "Get up and go to the street called Straight Street. Find the house of Judas. Ask for a man named Saul from the city of Tarsus. He is there now, praying. Saul has seen a vision. In it a man named Ananias comes to him and lays his hands on him. Then he sees again."

God loves us. And He can change anyone! Saul loved God, but he didn't believe Jesus was God's Son. So he did not like the people who loved Jesus and wanted to obey Him. Saul wanted to throw them in jail! He was traveling to the city of Damascus to look for more of Jesus' followers to arrest.

While he was on his way to the city, he saw a very bright light. Saul was blinded by the light. That light was Jesus! Jesus told Saul that when he was mean to His followers, it was like he was being mean to Jesus Himself. Jesus told Saul to go to the city and someone would help him.

In the city there was a man named Ananias. He loved the Lord very much. While Ananias was praying, Jesus told him that Saul was coming. He wanted Ananias to help Saul. Ananias had heard about how Saul was mean to the people who loved Jesus. Ananias had a choice to make: trust and obey the Lord, or be afraid and not help Saul.

Ananias obeyed the Lord and went to pray with Saul. Then Saul could see again. Saul was very sorry for hurting Jesus' followers and did not hurt them anymore. Now Saul loved Jesus and told everyone about Him. What about you?

Pray with Me

Dear God, help me be nice to others. Help me spend time with You and love You with all my heart. Amen.

Take It with You . . .

I will be like Ananias and let Jesus show me how I can love others.

Missy Benfield
Prospect Baptist Church, Albemarle, NC

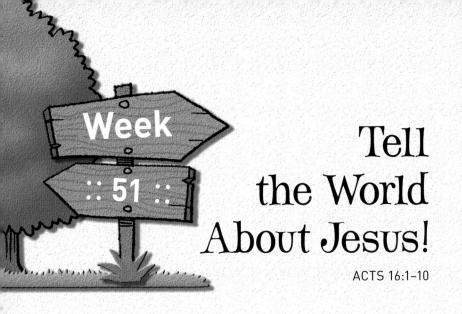

Tell the World About Jesus!

ACTS 16:1–10

Paul came to Derbe and Lystra. A follower named Timothy was there. Timothy's mother was Jewish and a believer. His father was a Greek. The brothers in Lystra and Iconium respected Timothy and said good things about him. Paul wanted Timothy to travel with him. But all the Jews living in that area knew that Timothy's father was Greek. So Paul circumcised Timothy to please the Jews. Paul and the men with him traveled from town to town. They gave the decisions made by the apostles and elders in Jerusalem for the people to obey. So the churches became stronger in the faith and grew larger every day. Paul and the men with him went through the areas of Phrygia and Galatia. The Holy Spirit did not let them preach the Good News in Asia. When they came near the country of Mysia, they tried to go

into Bithynia. But the Spirit of Jesus did not let them. So they passed by Mysia and went to Troas. That night Paul had a vision. In the vision, a man from Macedonia came to him. The man stood there and begged, "Come over to Macedonia. Help us!" After Paul had seen the vision, we immediately prepared to leave for Macedonia. We understood that God had called us to tell the Good News to those people.

Paul—who used to be called Saul—went into the
towns of Derbe and Lystra and met a man named
Timothy, who would travel with him and tell
people about Jesus. They went to many cities, and
many people believed what they said about how
Jesus loved them, died for them, and rose from
the dead to save them.

Paul was faithful to learn and know God's will
for his life, and also to do what God wanted him
to do. He started to go to one place to tell people
about Jesus, but the Holy Spirit led him to go to
Macedonia instead. He had a dream of a man in
Macedonia saying, "Please come help us." Paul
understood that God was telling him where He
wanted Paul to go, and Paul obeyed. Paul and
Timothy loved God and wanted to tell as many

people as they could about Jesus and how much He loved them.

Just like Paul and Timothy, we can know what God wants us to do by reading the Bible and talking to God. God tells us in His Word how we are supposed to live so that we can make Him happy. One of the things God wants us to do is tell other people about His Son, Jesus. Tell someone about Jesus today!

Pray with Me

Dear Lord, thank You for loving me and for giving me the Bible so that I will always know what You want me to do. Amen.

Take It with You . . .

I will obey God and do what He wants me to do. I will tell my friends about Jesus!

H. Marshall Thompson, Jr.
Riverstone Community Church, Jacksonville, FL

Someone Is Listening

ACTS 16:20–21, 23–34

They brought Paul and Silas to the Roman rulers and said, "These men are Jews and are making trouble in our city. They are teaching things that are not right for us as Romans to do." . . .

After being severely beaten, Paul and Silas were thrown into jail. The jailer was ordered to guard them carefully. When he heard this order, he put them far inside the jail. He pinned down their feet between large blocks of wood.

About midnight Paul and Silas were praying and singing songs to God. The other prisoners were listening to them. Suddenly, there was a big earthquake. It was so strong that it shook the foundation of the jail. Then all the doors of the jail broke open. All the prisoners were freed from their chains. The jailer woke up and saw that the jail doors were open. He thought that the prisoners

had already escaped. So he got his sword and was about to kill himself. But Paul shouted, "Don't hurt yourself! We are all here!"

The jailer told someone to bring a light. Then he ran inside. Shaking with fear, he fell down before Paul and Silas. Then he brought them outside and said, "Men, what must I do to be saved?"

They said to him, "Believe in the Lord Jesus and you will be saved—you and all the people in your house." So Paul and Silas told the message of the Lord to the jailer and all the people in his house. At that hour of the night the jailer took Paul and Silas and washed their wounds. Then he and all his people were baptized immediately. After this the jailer took Paul and Silas home and gave them food. He and his family were very happy because they now believed in God.

Have you ever been blamed for something you did not do? Paul and Silas were a long way from home telling people about Jesus. One day some men told the Roman soldiers that Paul and Silas were breaking the law. "These men should not be here," they said. "They are causing a lot of trouble for everyone."

Others heard what these people were saying and it made them mad, so they started hitting Paul and Silas. The soldiers threw Paul and Silas in jail, even though they had not done anything wrong. The soldiers ordered the jailer to guard Paul and Silas carefully, so the jailor put them in the part of the jail where they would be all alone. But they really were not all alone—God was with them.

Then the jailer put Paul's and Silas's hands and feet in locks so they could not move. Paul and Silas did not complain. They did not get mad or pout.

In the middle of the night, they sang to the Lord, praising His awesome and wonderful name. God was so happy with them. He was not the only one listening, though. The other prisoners heard too.

Then God sent an earthquake, and the foundation of the jail shook. Even the chains fell off Paul and Silas. But no one ran away. The jailer was afraid that all of the prisoners had left, and he knew he would be in big trouble. But Paul called out, "We are all here!"

The jailer fell to his feet and wanted to know more about their God. So Paul and Silas told the jailer and his whole family about Jesus. That very night, the jailer and his family believed in Jesus, and they were baptized.

Pray with Me

Lord, thank You for always being with me and never leaving me alone. I pray I will feel and act the way that makes You happy. Amen.

Take It with You

I will remember that I am never all alone. I will act in a way that causes others to want to know Jesus.

Dr. Michael Cloer
Englewood Baptist Church, Rocky Mount, NC

Contributers

ANDERSON, PASTOR TIM
  Clements Baptist Church, Athens, AL . . . . Week 25
Benfield, Missy
  Prospect Baptist Church, Albemarle, NC . . . . Week 50
BOWERS, NORMA
  Flint-Groves Baptist Church, Gastonia, NC . . . . Week 45
BOWMAN, DR. J. KIE
  Hyde Park Baptist Church, Austin, TX . . . . Week 34
BRIDGES, CHRIS
  Calvary Church, Clearwater, FL . . . . Week 10
BULLARD, PASTOR KELLY
  Temple Baptist Church, Fayetteville, NC . . . . Week 42
CARSWELL, DEANNA HUNT
  First Baptist Church Woodstock, Woodstock, GA . . . . . Week 23
CHENAULT, ANNE
  First Baptist Church, Chipley, FL . . . . Week 37
CLOER, DR. MICHAEL
  Englewood Baptist Church, Rocky Mount, NC . . . . . . Week 52
COOPER, BRADY AND AMY
  New Vision Baptist Church, Murfreesboro, TN . . . . . . Week 28
COX, MARY
  North Metro Baptist Church, Lawrenceville, GA . . . . . Week 35
CROOK, PASTOR JEFF
  Blackshear Place Baptist Church, Flowery Branch, GA . . Week 14
DeTELLIS, TIM
  New Missions, Orlando, FL . . . . Week 17

DIXON, AMY
    Liberty Baptist Church, Dublin, GA . . . . Week 19

DOOLEY, DR. ADAM
    Sunnyvale First Baptist Church, Dallas, TX . . . . Week 18

EDWARDS, DAVID
    David Edwards Productions, Inc., Oklahoma City, OK . . Week 20

EPPL, MARY
    First Baptist Orlando, Orlando, FL . . . . Week 38

ETHRIDGE, DR. GRANT
    Liberty Baptist Church, Hampton, VA . . . . Week 21

EWING, DR. MELISSA
    First Baptist Church, McKinney, TX . . . . Week 29

FLEMING, DR. DAVID
    Champion Forest Baptist Church, Houston, TX . . . . . . Week 41

FLOCKHART, STEVE
    New Season Church, Hiram, GA . . . . Week 27

FLOYD, DR. RONNIE
    Cross Church, Northwest Arkansas . . . . Week 36

FOSSETT, MACEY
    Fossett Ministries, Dalton, GA . . . . Week 15

HARTZELL, RYAN
    The Creek Church, London, KY . . . . Week 43

HIXSON, HOLLIE
    Cross Point Church, Nashville, TN . . . . Week 40

HOLLOWAY, REV. AARON M.
    Burnt Hickory Baptist Church, Powder Springs, GA . . . Week 26

HOOD, ANALISA
    Mobberly Baptist Church, Longview, TX . . . . Week 33

HUNLEY, BEN

    Second Baptist Church, Warner Robins, GA . . . . Week 16

HUNT, DR. JOHNNY

    First Baptist Church Woodstock, Woodstock, GA . . . . . Week 1

HUNT, JANET

    First Baptist Church Woodstock, Woodstock, GA . . . . . Week 30

KUBISH, DAN AND DEBBIE

    NewSpring Church, Wichita, KS . . . . Week 22

LATHAM, DR. PATRICK

    First Baptist Church Lawton-Fort Sill, Lawton, OK . . . Week 44

LAYWELL, DR. D'ANN, *North Richland Hills*

    Baptist Church, North Richland Hills, TX . . . . Week 39

LEE, JUDY

    There's Hope America Ministries, Cumming, GA . . . . . Week 49

MERCER, PAM

    CrossLife Church, Oviedo, FL . . . . Week 2

MERRITT, DR. JAMES

    Cross Pointe Church, Duluth, GA . . . . Week 24

NUNN, DENNIS

    Every Believer a Witness Ministries, Dallas, GA . . . . . Week 12

PITMAN, DR. BOB

    Bob Pitman Ministries, Muscle Shoals, AL . . . . Week 6

PURVIS, KIMBERLY

    FBC Temple Terrace, Temple Terrace, FL . . . . Week 11

RICHARDSON, REV. DAVID

    First Baptist Church, Creedmoor, NC . . . . Week 46

SCHREVE, DEBBIE

    First Baptist Church, Texarkana, TX . . . . Week 9

TATE, DR. BENNY
  Rock Springs Church, Milner, GA . . . . Week 4
THOMAS, DR. PHIL
  Shiloh Baptist Church, Fort Gaines, GA . . . . Week 48
THOMPSON, JR., H. MARSHALL
  Riverstone Community Church, Jacksonville, FL . . . . . Week 51
THOMPSON, DR. LARRY
  First Fort Lauderdale, Fort Lauderdale, FL . . . . Week 8
TRAYLOR, DR. TED
  Olive Baptist Church, Pensacola, FL . . . . Week 7
WALKER, SUZANNE
  Mobberly Baptist Church, Longview, TX . . . . Week 33
WELBORN, PASTOR JOHN
  Crosslink Community Church, Harrisonburg, VA . . . . Week 47
WHITE, ANN
  In Grace Ministries, Marietta, GA . . . . Week 32
WHITSON, DR. MIKE
  First Baptist Church Indian Trail, Indian Trail, NC . . . Week 3
WHITT, DR. BRAD
  Abilene Baptist Church, Martinez, GA . . . . Week 5
WILTON, DR. DON
  First Baptist Church, Spartanburg, SC . . . . Week 31
ZINN, DR. ROB
  Immanuel Baptist Church, Highland, CA . . . . Week 13

Books of the Bible

Old Testament

Genesis

Exodus

Leviticus

Numbers

Deuteronomy

Joshua

Judges

Ruth

1 Samuel

2 Samuel

1 Kings

2 Kings

1 Chronicles

2 Chronicles

Ezra

Nehemiah

Esther

Job

Psalms

Proverbs

Ecclesiastes

Song of Solomon

Isaiah

Jeremiah

Lamentations

Ezekiel

Daniel

Hosea

Joel

Amos

Obadiah

Jonah

Micah

Nahum

Habakkuk

Zephaniah

Haggai

Zechariah

Malachi

New Testament

Matthew
Mark
Luke
John
Acts
Romans
1 Corinthians
2 Corinthians
Galatians
Ephesians

Philippians
Colossians
1 Thessalonians
2 Thessalonians
1 Timothy
2 Timothy
Titus
Philemon
Hebrews
James

1 Peter
2 Peter
1 John
2 John
3 John
Jude
Revelation

Selected Verses from the Book of Proverbs

Remember the Lord in everything you do.
    And he will give you success.

—PROVERBS 3:6

Whenever you are able,
    do good to people who need help.

—PROVERBS 3:27

Always remember what you have been taught.
　　Don't let go of it.
Keep safe all that you have learned.
　　It is the most important thing in your life.

—PROVERBS 4:13

A person who quickly gets angry causes trouble.
　　But a person who controls his temper stops a
　　　quarrel.

—PROVERBS 15:18

Even a child is known by his behavior.
　　His actions show if he is innocent and good.

—PROVERBS 20:11

A person who is careful about what he says
　　keeps himself out of trouble.

—PROVERBS 21:23

"Every word of God can be trusted.
　　He protects those who come to
　　　him for safety."

—PROVERBS 30:5

The Twelve Disciples

Peter

James, son of Zebedee

John

Andrew

Philip

Bartholomew

Matthew

Thomas

James, son of Alphaeus

Thaddaeus

Simon the Zealot

Judas Iscariot

"For God loved the world so much that he gave his only Son. God gave his Son so that whoever believes in him may not be lost, but have eternal life."

—JOHN 3:16